Grammatical Concepts 101 for Biblical Greek

Grammatical Concepts 101

for Biblical Greek

*Learning Biblical Greek Grammatical Concepts
through English Grammar*

GARY A. LONG

ℬ
Baker Academic

a division of Baker Publishing Group
Grand Rapids, Michigan

© 2006 by Gary A. Long

Published by Baker Academic
a division of Baker Publishing Group
PO Box 6287, Grand Rapids, MI 49516-6287
www.bakeracademic.com

Baker Academic edition published 2020
ISBN 978-0-8010-4693-3

Previously published in 2006 by Hendrickson Publishers

Printed in the United States of America

The Library of Congress has cataloged the original edition as follows:
Long, Gary A. (Gary Alan), 1959–
    Grammatical concepts 101 for biblical Greek : learning Biblical Greek grammatical con-
  cepts through English grammar / Gary A. Long.
       p. cm.
  Includes bibliographical references and index.
  ISBN 1-56563-106-3 (alk. paper)
  1. Greek language, Biblical—Grammar. 2. English language—Grammar. 3. Bible.
N.T.—Language, style. I. Title.
  PA817.L66 2006
  487'.4—dc22   2006041188

For my father and the memory of my mother

JIM AND VELMA LONG

TABLE OF CONTENTS

PART I: FOUNDATIONS

PART II: BUILDING BLOCKS

PART III: THE CLAUSE AND BEYOND

LIST OF FIGURES

ACKNOWLEDGMENTS

Motivated students who have walked the same path as I in wanting to learn biblical languages have been the inspiration behind this book and its earlier sister on Biblical Hebrew.[1] I hope they will find this volume the help I want it to be for them.

I had the good fortune of writing a portion of this book while on sabbatical at the Department of Ancient Studies at the University of Stellenbosch, South Africa. I am most grateful to its faculty members. In particular, I cannot express enough thanks to my friend and colleague, Christo van der Merwe. It is he who graciously opened the door and saw to my professional needs there. I especially found it meaningful to come each day and sit within the department's collections of the late professors F. C. Fensham and P. F. D. Weiss. I also thank H. Huismann, the department's administrator, for her help. Bernard Heesen of the University's IT team graciously saw to my laptop and other IT needs. Cecilia Vockins, also of IT, has my thanks. From everyone at the university, I felt warm South African hospitality.

I also found warm hospitality from Johan and Ode Krige, innkeepers of the Caledon Villa Guest House in Stellenbosch, and their pleasant staff. Caledon Villa's Jan Cats apartment allowed my family and me to live within and embrace the very heart of Stellenbosch and the whole of the Western Cape. One would have a difficult time finding a more breathtaking and visitor-friendly area of the world than South Africa's Western Cape.

I am indebted to the English Grammar Series (Olivia and Hill Press) for the idea of illustrating English alongside a language to be learned. I have been helped by a number of my colleagues at Bethel University. Don Alexander, Michael Holmes, and especially Mark Reasoner and Lidija Novakovic carefully read several chapters and offered fine criticism. A Bethel University Alumni Faculty Grant helped

---

[1] Gary A. Long, *Grammatical Concepts 101 for Biblical Hebrew: Learning Biblical Hebrew Grammatical Concepts through English Grammar* (Peabody, Mass.: Hendrickson, 2002).

to underwrite my time in South Africa and to compensate one of my fine students, Justin Buol, for his careful reading of earlier drafts. Shirley Decker-Lucke, of Hendrickson, and the fine personnel there have guided this project through to publication with efficiency and grace. Errors and insufficiencies that still remain, of course, are entirely my own doing.

This book is testimony to the depth of my parents' love, provision, and encouragement throughout my life. Though I am reminded each and every day, as I look at myself, of evidence to the contrary, their own example of doing one's best and pursuing excellence are hallmarks I trust are engrained in some fashion within me. A lifetime dedicated to humanitarian and religious endeavors in places such as India, Bangladesh, and the Philippines brought a bounty of peaks and valleys. It was in those valleys—*years* at a time!—that their true character shined. Inclined more toward hands-on humanitarian and parish work, my parents found themselves, uncomfortably, in key administrative roles over a seminary and a college. The appointment was to be one brief, interim year. Four years would pass. I keep a memento of that valley in my office; I asked my dad for it recently. It's a very plain name plaque for a desktop: Rev. James W. Long, President, Administrative Dean, Business Manager. And that was only for the seminary! My mom had one similar. As my parents would reflect in retirement on those years, I heard them often say that precisely because they would have preferred to have been elsewhere, they worked all the harder! While I was writing this book, cancer took my mom. With family around her, moments before the nurse started the morphine drip that would render her oblivious to the world, she looked at all of us. "I've lived a *great* life" were her words through a contented smile. I've lived enough of life to fully understand the import of those words and how unachievable such a declaration can be for many. I have witnessed parents of true character. I have watched parents give their absolute best—always. I have observed parents who successfully lived life without regrets. To you, dad, and mom's memory, this book is dedicated.

The Twin Cities, Minnesota   *G. A. LONG*
January 2006

INTRODUCTION

Designed to complement standard teaching grammars, this book assists the entry-level Biblical Greek student in learning basic grammatical concepts no single *teaching* grammar treats adequately and no *reference* grammar explains plainly enough for many beginning students. We revisit English grammar to accomplish this. After several years of teaching a variety of ancient languages, I recognize that most of my students have been learning two languages at the same time: the ancient language, of course, *and* the grammar and grammatical concepts of English, often forgotten.

I have written the book for a learner who has had little or no formal study of grammar. The language, therefore, strives for simplicity wherever possible. Some will find the language, at times, simplistic, overly so. I define nouns, for example, as words that name, rather than according to formal and functional criteria such as case and number inflection, syntactic functions, distribution (they follow prepositions but not modals), etc. Others might find the language, at times, a bit of a challenge. You, the reader, will see abundant English and Greek examples illustrating each concept, most of them *visually* analyzed. A gloss (a literal, word-by-word English equivalent of the Greek) and translation assist the comprehension of the Greek examples.

Sometimes within my discussion of English grammar I will refer to particular constructions as "prestige" and "colloquial." Like many languages, English has an acrolect, a basilect, and points in between. An *acrolect* is the prestige variety of a language; a *basilect* is the colloquial form. Within the halls of the academy, the commonest surroundings I envision for this textbook, I have thought it pedagogically useful to use English's acrolect, its prestige forms, while pointing out pertinent colloquial ones. The academy, on occasion, still expects the acrolect of its students.

The concepts in this book are arranged from the more basic to the more involved. "Part I: Foundations" contains concepts that lie at the very foundation of language. "Part II: Building Blocks" treats concepts in an order similar to many teaching grammars. Here the learner can augment a teaching grammar's presentation. "Part III: The Clause and Beyond" introduces the learner to the higher levels of language.

This resource is not comprehensive in subject matter, and it does not show the full variety of ways Biblical Greek may convey a particular concept. Many of the concepts I address are more completely analyzed in the many fine Biblical Greek reference grammars. Consult them as you become more familiar with grammar and as your ability to read Greek increases over time.[2] They are *indispensable*.

TIPS FOR LEARNING BIBLICAL GREEK

1. **Memory.** Your memory plays an important role in learning a language. You will spend many hours memorizing vocabulary, paradigms, grammatical rules, and the like. Here are some thoughts that may help you with those tasks.

   - Divide the lesson into learnable sections.

   - Read each section aloud several times.

   - Rewrite the section word for word or in your own words.

   - Compare what you have written with the textbook.

2. **Vocabulary.** Each of us brings different abilities to the learning process. In learning a language, you will likely learn a lot about yourself—what works for you, what does not. Some strategies will work, some will not. Try different approaches and stick with anything that helps you learn. Here is what other learners have tried.

   - Write each word on a blank vocabulary card: Greek on one side, English on the other.

   - Use cards of different color to assist you with helpful classifications: gender of nominals (one color for masculine, one for feminine nouns, and

---

[2] For example, Daniel B. Wallace, *Greek Grammar beyond the Basics: An Exegetical Syntax of the New Testament* (Grand Rapids, Mich.: Zondervan, 1996).

another for neuter), or parts of speech (one color for verbs, another for adjectives).

- Flip through the cards reading the Greek aloud, then think of the English gloss (= literal translation). Flip through the cards, reading the English and saying the Greek aloud. Shuffle the cards so that you do not become too reliant on order and placement.

- Many Biblical Greek words have a foundation, or *root*, or, more linguistically, *lex(eme)* (see definition under LINGUISTIC HIERARCHIES, beginning on p. 3), which some find helpful to view as a core meaning. Most all words that share this foundation are related in meaning—they share a *linkedness* or *connectedness.* For example, γεν 'become, give birth' is the foundation that underlies γονεύς *parent,* and γενεά *generation,* and γένος *race,* etc. You of course see the connection. Try grouping vocabulary cards by their common foundation/root.

  Be attentive to recurring patterns in words. They can help you identify, for example, adjectives from common nouns and present verb forms from future forms. David Alan Black's introductory grammar emphasizes this strategy, which keeps rote memorization to a minimum.[3]

3. **Assignments.** Keep up with the assignments. Do not let yourself fall behind. Morale, to say nothing of grades, can nose-dive when you do not keep pace.

---

[3] David Alan Black, *Learn to Read New Testament Greek* (Nashville: Broadman, 1993).

Part I
Foundations

LINGUISTIC HIERARCHIES

A helpful way to view language is to see it as a fusion of the abstract (EMIC) with the tangible (ETIC). Think of a word in your head. Now think of an entire sentence. Think of a few more things you could say. No one knows what you have just thought. This *emic* realm of language is abstract, not tangible, existing only in your mind. The emic is the conceptual realm of language.

Now say aloud what you had in your mind, or take a pen and write it down. This *etic* realm of language is physically represented when one speaks or writes (or gestures, if one communicates through sign language). Language is *physically* produced through sounds (*phones*) or writing symbols (*graphs*). These sounds and written symbols are the building blocks of words, phrases, and clauses that can be conveyed to another person.

We can break down language into building blocks or hierarchies. Each of the following units, listed from smallest to largest (bottom to top in figure 1), has an emic and etic realm. The term *expression* is convenient to refer to a written or oral articulation of language at the level of word or higher when I do not have a specific level in mind.

EMIC	ETIC	
emic discourse or text	etic discourse or text	
emic paragraph	etic paragraph	
emic sentence	etic sentence or utterance	Expression
emic clause	etic clause	
emic phrase	etic phrase	
emic word lexical item	etic word or lexical item	
lexeme	lex	
morpheme	morph	
phoneme	phone	

Figure 1: Linguistic Hierarchies

PHONE(ME)   is a sound or speech unit that is psychologically a single unit and that makes a difference. Make a /z/ sound, as in *zebra*. Now make a /v/ sound, as in *victory*. The sounds or speech units /z/ and /v/ are psychologically each a single unit and each makes a difference. The first word, after all, makes no sense if we say *vebra;* and *zictory* is equally nonsensical. βόνος does not clearly communicate that you mean to say μόνος. Linguists use slashed lines to represent phonemes. These abstract units often have variations when articulated as phones. Sounds next to each other, whether another consonant or a vowel, can affect each other. These variations are known as **ALLOPHONES**. For example, hold your hand close to your mouth and say the words *pin* and *spin*. Notice that the /p/ of *pin* includes a more explosive burst of air than the /p/ of *spin*.

MORPH(EME)   is the *smallest* or *minimal* block of language that is *meaningful* and recurrent for word-building in a language. The notion of *meaningful* is important. A phone(me) is the smallest block but it does not convey meaning. What, after all, does /b/ mean? It does not *mean* anything. All sorts of concepts are conveyed in morphemes: plurality, singularity, tense, gender, etc. Morphemes may have variations known as **ALLOMORPHS**. For example, the morpheme 'plural of a noun' has the allomorphs -*s* (*cats*), -*z* (*lids*), and -*əz* (*forces*). In Greek, the morpheme 'opposite' or 'instead of' is conveyed through the allomorphs ἀντί (before smooth breathing) and ἀνθ' (before rough breathing).

LEX(EME)   is the typically foundational element of a word or lexical item. The idea of a lex(eme) is not the easiest to comprehend. In English it is typically represented as the dictionary form of any word. For example, a person learning English may encounter the word *kicked* in a text; the dictionary will have the word entered simply as *kick*. *Kick*, represented on the page as *k-i-c-k*, is the *lex*, while the (emic) concept behind the word, 'kick', is the *lexeme*. The notion of lex(eme) is similar in Biblical Greek. The lexeme 'reverence' is represented in the lex ἁγ, which underlies ἅγιος *holy* and ἁγιασμός *sanctification*. Commonly, Biblical Greek grammarians give the label *root* to what I am here calling a lex(eme). Unlike English, however, Biblical Greek has some roots that are *not* a simple dictionary form.

WORD   is a language building block composed of a lexeme and all morphemes. For example, the etic lexical item or word *kicked* is composed, in part, of the lexeme 'kick' plus the morpheme 'past tense', reflected in the morph *-ed*. Parsing is in fact accounting for the lexemic and morphemic composition of a word. The etic verb form φερώμεθα *let us press on* is composed of the lexeme 'bear, carry', represented in the lex φερ, plus the morphemes 'present', 'first person', 'plural', 'subjunctive', etc.

PHRASE   is a language unit referring to a string of words (a *syntagm*)— two or more—that does *not* involve predication (see **PREDI- CATE/PREDICATION**, p. 199). Think of a **PREDICATE** as a comment about a subject. A phrase does *not* have a subject and a predicate together.

ἐν Χριστῷ in Christ

CLAUSE   is a language unit referring to a string of words (a *syntagm*) that *does* involve predication. It involves a **COMMENT**, very commonly about a subject, which is *usually* present. See **CLAUSE**, p. 193.

μακάριοι	οἱ	πτωχοὶ	τῷ	πνεύματι	Blessed are the poor
blessed	the	poor	in-the	spirit	in spirit.

Matthew 5:3

A subject (or *topic*) and predicate (or *comment*) are together in the example. Here the subject is "the poor in spirit." The predicate or comment about the subject is "are blessed." "The poor in spirit . . . ." What is the comment about them? They "are blessed."

SENTENCE

is a language unit referring to a string of words that includes predication and that in Biblical Greek is typically composed of one independent clause or more and all modifying subordinate clauses. By this definition, a sentence composed of only one independent unmodified clause is both a clause and a sentence. (The above example from Matthew 5:3 fits this case.)

PARAGRAPH

is a language unit that in Biblical Greek is typically composed of two or more sentences usually with a similar topic. Two or more sentences may be equally prominent, or prominent sentences may occur along with modifying sentences (such as reason or result).

DISCOURSE

is the highest of the linguistic hierarchies, typically composed of any "chunk" of text above the level of a sentence. It may be equal to a paragraph but is typically more. See **DISCOURSE ANALYSIS,** p. 211.

SOUND PRODUCTION

Why should we be concerned with sound production? Nobody today converses in Biblical Greek, after all—a fair question.

The New Testament's audience primarily *heard* rather than *read* the text. The sounds of Biblical Greek can affect not only spelling but word choice. Reading aloud as you study Biblical Greek will help you learn it faster and understand better what you are reading. It will also help you appreciate stylistic features of the text that usually are lost in translation—for example, the alliteration in Hebrews 1:1–2, which seeks to match the alliteration in the opening lines of Homer's *Odyssey*.

Speech **SOUNDS** or **SEGMENTS** are the fundamental components of a spoken language. Created along the **VOCAL TRACT** (the area between the vocal folds and lips), they tend to be classified according to the amount of obstruction involved in producing them. Vowel sounds are generally produced with less obstruction than consonantal sounds. The following discussion has Biblical Greek primarily in mind.

The classifications and sound descriptions I use below follow a standard North American "academic" pronunciation used in many teaching grammars. This more-or-less standard pronunciation tries to approximate, though imprecisely, an Athenian or Attic dialect in the classical period (5th–4th cent. B.C.E.). Ancient Greek had a *wide* range of dialects producing a *wide* variation of sounds for the letters of the alphabet. We can only approximate.

Do not think that those living in Greece today will easily understand your academic Greek should you wish to impress them on your next trip. Modern Greek's pronunciation is quite different.

During the first century C.E., the Greek pronunciation underlying the New Testament, as you might now imagine, differed from the academic. If this interests you, take a look at a helpful discussion offered by David Alan Black or Daniel Wallace.[4]

CONSONANTS

PLACE OF ARTICULATION, **MANNER OF ARTICULATION**, and **VOICING** are concepts commonly associated with producing consonants.

PLACE OF ARTICULATION

The place of articulation is the point in the vocal tract where the greatest constriction or obstruction occurs (see figure 2 below, p. 11). The Biblical Greek consonants include the following articulatory places.

Labials	sound formed by the lips
Bilabials	sound formed by the two lips together: β, μ, π, ψ
Labiodentals	sound formed by the lower lip tucked just behind the upper front teeth: φ
Labioalveolars	sound formed by the lips and at the alveolar ridge: ρ
Labiovelars	sound formed by the lips and at the velum: υ (when it *ends* a diphthong)
Dentals	sound formed with the tip of the tongue touching the back of the upper front teeth (we are uncertain whether any ancient Greek consonant is precisely a dental, though some grammars classify some as such; we therefore classify such consonants as alveolars)
Interdentals	consonants formed with the tip of the tongue placed between the teeth: θ

---

[4] David Alan Black, *Linguistics for Students of New Testament Greek: A Survey of Basic Concepts and Applications* (2d ed.; Grand Rapids, Mich.: Baker Books, 1995), 38–40; Wallace, *Greek Grammar,* 12–30.

Alveolars	sound formed with the tip of the tongue raised to the bony ridge immediately behind the teeth, the alveolar ridge: δ, ζ, λ, ν, σ, τ
Alveopalatals	sound formed with the tip of the tongue raised to the bony ridge immediately behind the teeth and at the hard palate: ι (when it *ends* a diphthong)
Velars	sound formed with the center and dorsum of the tongue raised to the velum or soft palate: γ, nasal-γ (immediately before γ, κ, ξ, χ), κ, ξ, χ (here you may note that γ becomes a nasal [= nasal-γ] before any velar)
Pharyngeals	sound formed in the upper pharyngeal cavity (Greek has no pharyngeal *consonant,* but the "rough breathing" sound is pharyngeal): ʽ
Glottals	sound formed in the glottal region, the opening between the vocal folds (Greek has no glottal *consonant,* but the "smooth breathing" sound is glottal; this symbol, associated with words that begin with vowels, represents the same sound that begins vowel-initial words such as *orange* or *apple* in English): ʼ

MANNER OF ARTICULATION

The vocal tract can affect airflow. Manner of articulation refers to the manner or way that the sound is produced, usually in terms of the amount of constriction the airflow encounters. Biblical Greek has OBSTRUENTS and the SONORANTS.

Obstruent	a distinctive feature that characterizes speech sound when airflow is constricted
Plosive/Stop	obstruent sound made by temporarily blocking the airflow completely: β, δ, γ, κ, π, τ

Fricative   obstruent sound in which the airflow is channeled
                       through a narrow opening in the speech path: θ, φ,
                       χ, and ῾ ("rough breathing")

                       Within the fricative category you should take note of
                       SIBILANTS. Higher frequency energy is required to
                       produce sibilants, giving them a hissing sound. The
                       sibilant is σ.[5]

Affricative   obstruent sound in which the airflow for a single
                       consonant consists of a plosive/stop followed by a
                       secondary fricative release: ζ, ξ, ψ

Trill   obstruent sound where vibration occurs, or, more
                       specifically, where one part of the vocal tract rapidly
                       taps another: ρ (some pronounce ρ as an alveolar to
                       which trill is added [the tip or apex of the tongue
                       taps the alveolar ridge]; this is most likely the pro-
                       nunciation in Classical Greek)

Sonorant   a distinctive feature that characterizes speech sound
                       whose articulation is not so narrow that the airflow
                       across the glottis is appreciably inhibited

Nasal   sonorant sound made with a lowered velum, thus
                       engaging the natural resonance of the nasal pas-
                       sages—the oral cavity is closed so that air flows
                       through the nasal cavity: nasal-γ (immediately be-
                       fore γ, κ, ξ, χ), μ, ν

---

[5] Some grammars teach that *word*-initial ζ is pronounced as a sibilant; *within* a word those same grammars describe ζ as an affricative. Those grammars appear to be reflecting a common dialect underlying the Greek of the first century C.E., not the earlier dialect the academic pronunciation tries to approximate. For example, Ray Summers, *Essentials of New Testament Greek* (rev. Thomas Sawyer; rev. ed; Nashville: Broadman & Holman, 1995), 1; Gerald L. Stevens, *New Testament Greek* (2d ed.; Lanham, Md.: University Press of America, 1997), 2.

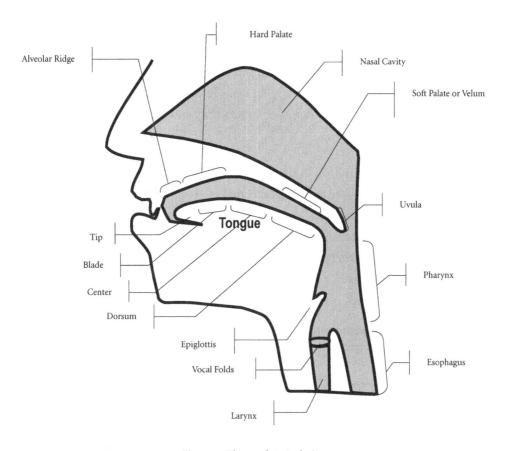

Figure 2: Places of Articulation

Liquid   sonorant sound in which the speech path is neither closed off nor constricted to a degree that produces friction

Under the label of liquids, Biblical Greek has a

     Lateral   consonant, λ, where the tip of the tongue is raised to the alveolar ridge but the sides of the tongue are down, permitting the air to flow laterally over the sides of the tongue.

11

Glide		sonorant vowel-like sound: ρ (Americans commonly pronounce ρ as they do their consonant *r,* that is, as a glide with retroflex, where the bottom surface of the tongue's tip is in close proximity to the alveolar ridge); ι, υ (when they *end* a diphthong)

VOICING

Voicing refers to the vibration of the vocal folds during the production of a sound. If the vocal folds are tense and the airflow from the lungs forces them to vibrate, the consonantal sounds are VOICED. If the air flows freely through the relaxed vocal folds into the supraglottal (above the glottis) speech organs, the consonantal sounds are VOICELESS. Put several of your fingers on the front of your throat. Pronounce /v/ as in *victory;* now pronounce /f/ as in *fine.* Did you feel the vibration associated with pronouncing *victory* and the lack of it in saying *fine?*

Here are the Greek consonants that have voicing: β, γ, nasal-γ (immediately before γ, κ, ξ, χ), δ, ζ, λ, μ, ν, ρ. The rest are voiceless: θ, κ, ξ, π, σ, τ, φ, χ, ψ.

We are ready to summarize the consonants.

	PLACE	VOICING	MANNER
β	bilabial	voiced	plosive
γ	velar	voiced	plosive
nasal-γ	velar	voiced	nasal
δ	alveolar	voiced	plosive
ζ	alveolar	voiced	affricative[6]
θ	interdental	voiceless	fricative
κ	velar	voiceless	plosive

---

[6] Evidence supports that in addition to this [dz] sound, ζ was pronounced in Classical Athenian/Attic Greek as [zd].

12

λ	alveolar	voiced	lateral
μ	bilabial	voiced	nasal
ν	alveolar	voiced	nasal
ξ	velar	voiceless	affricative
π	bilabial	voiceless	plosive
ρ	labioalveolar retroflex	voiced	glide
σ ς	alveolar	voiceless	fricative
τ	alveolar	voiceless	plosive
φ	labiodental	voiceless	fricative
χ	velar	voiceless	fricative
ψ	bilabial	voiceless	affricative

Figure 3: Phonetic Classification of Consonants

VOWELS

Vowel sounds have little obstruction in Biblical Greek. For vowels we distinguish QUALITY (or TIMBRE), the difference in vowel sound production along the speech path, and QUANTITY (or DURATION or LENGTH), the time spent in producing the vowel sound. Further, TONGUE POSITION and LIP POSITION are important factors.

A SIMPLE (or PURE) vowel refers to one with a single sound. A DIPHTHONG is a sequence of two sounds consisting of a simple vowel plus a glide sound. Greek diphthongs end either with ι or υ. They produce a glide sound: an alveopalatal, voiced glide (the sound of *y* in *buy*) and a labiovelar, voiced glide (the sound of *w* in *now*) respectively.

TONGUE POSITION

Here one may note (1) the height of the tongue and (2) the part of the tongue employed. The tongue height may be HIGH, MID, or LOW. High vowels are also

13

known as CLOSE vowels; low ones are OPEN. The part of the tongue used may be the FRONT (tip and blade), CENTER, and BACK (dorsum). For example, the vowel sound in the English word

beet is high and front;

boot is high and back;

hot is low and back;

boat is mid and back;

bought is between mid and low and back;

cup is mid and central.

LIP POSITION

Vowel sounds differ depending on whether the lips are rounded. For example, in the previous paragraph, the vowel in *boot* was characterized as high and back, but it also entails lip rounding, while *hot* (low and back) has an unrounded vowel.

PUTTING THE PIECES TOGETHER: SIMPLE VOWELS

The charts below combine the features we use to categorize the simple vowels of Biblical Greek. Remember that simple vowels are ones with a *single* sound.

Biblical Greek has preserved seven symbols to represent seven simple vowel sounds: α, ε, η, ι, ο, υ, ω. Vowel *quantity* (or *length*) likely plays no role. In many languages, *long* vowels are ones, in part, that take *longer* to pronounce than short vowels. This was likely true of Greek for a time. Biblical Greek, however, does not maintain this *quantitative* difference. That is, we do not pronounce the long vowel η for a longer period of time than we pronounce the short vowel ε.

Many Biblical Greek teaching grammars talk of long and short vowels. Such classification, however, is based more on other differences such as *tenseness* (the muscular tension used) and vowel quality. Think of English. We do not have a formal system of pronouncing vowels for a shorter or longer period of time. We do, however, label the vowel sound in *pit* as "short" while the vowel sound in *peat* is "long." We pronounce the vowels, though, for the same amount of time!

This is similar to what the Greek grammars are doing in classifying Biblical Greek vowels.

Grammars tend to classify the simple vowels as short or long in the following fashion:

Short vowels	ε, ο
Long vowels	η, ω
Short *and* long vowels ("variable")	α, ι, υ

Figure 4: Long and Short Simple Vowels in Biblical Greek

The vowels in the bottom row, the "variable" vowels, are those that represent both a short and long vowel. In the academic pronunciation tradition, they have different *qualities/timbres* when short and long. The other four vowels, in the upper two rows, have only one quality/timbre.

We can classify the ten simple vowel qualities/timbres that the seven vowel letters represent in Biblical Greek:

Tongue Height	Part of Tongue		
	Front	**Center**	**Back**
	unrounded		rounded
Close ↑ **High**	ι (long) *machine* ι (short) *pit*		υ (long) *mood* υ (short) *book*
Mid	η *they* ε *bet*		ω *sold* ο *Gott, sought*[7]
↓ **Low** Open		α (short) *that* α (long) *father*	

Figure 5: Characteristics of Biblical Greek Simple Vowels

---

[7] If you know German, you understand the vowel sound in *Gott*. The English word "sought" is not quite accurate. If you pronounce the word, however, with your lips rounded, you come close.

15

PUTTING THE PIECES TOGETHER: DIPHTHONG VOWELS

A diphthong, remember, is a sequence of *two* sounds consisting of a simple vowel plus a glide sound (δίφθογγος *two sound*). Biblical Greek diphthongs end either with ι or υ. They produce a glide sound: an alveopalatal, voiced glide (the sound of *y* in *buy*) and a labiovelar, voiced glide (the sound of *w* in *now*) respectively. Thus, for example, the diphthong αι begins by producing the appropriate simple vowel sound associated with α and ends with an alveopalatal, voiced glide. What you should hear is a sound similar to how American English pronounces *eye*. The diphthong ευ begins by producing the simple vowel sound reflected by ε and ends with a labiovelar, voiced glide. The way that most American English speakers pronounce *feud* is close to what you should hear.

The Biblical Greek diphthongs are: αι

αυ

ει

ευ

ηυ

οι

ου

υι

Many grammars talk of *iota subscript* "diphthongs": ᾳ, ῃ, ῳ. In Biblical Greek these are vowels that once were diphthongs but have **MONOPHTHONGIZED**; that is, they have gone from *two* sounds to *one* simple vowel sound (μόνος *one* + φθόγγος *sound*): α, η, and ω, respectively.

SYLLABLE

A **SYLLABLE** is a sound or phonological unit composed of (1) an **ONSET**, (2) a **NU-CLEUS**, and sometimes (3) a **CODA**.

ENGLISH

In the English *bed,* /b/ is the onset, /ɛ/ is the nucleus, and /d/ is the coda.

BIBLICAL GREEK

Your primary grammar likely offers a version of the following overarching rule:

A Greek word has as many syllables as it has vowels (simple or diphthong).[8]

Here are some basic concepts associated with syllables.

➢ POSITION

A word in Greek may have one syllable or many. The last three syllable positions have specific labels. Moving from left to right, they are **ANTEPENULT**, **PENULT**, and **ULTIMA**. A single-syllable, or *monosyllabic,* word only has an *ultima.* A two-syllable, or *disyllabic,* word has a *penult* and *ultima.* A three-or-more-syllable, or *polysyllabic,* word has all three positions.

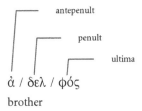

antepenult

penult

ultima

ἀ / δελ / φός
brother

➢ DIVISIBLE AND INDIVISIBLE CONSONANT CLUSTERS

Two consonants together commonly divide into separate syllables. The first consonant closes the first syllable; that is, it serves as the syllable's *coda.* The second consonant begins the next syllable, that is, it functions as the *onset.*

---

[8] For definitions of the simple and the diphthong vowel, see **SOUND PRODUCTION**, pp. 14 and 16 respectively.

βάλ / λω   βαπ / τί / ζω
throw   baptize

Clusters of particular consonants, though, do not split up. In particular, λ and ρ[9] and the nasals (μ, ν), when they are the second consonant, commonly do not divide.

- for example: βλ-, θλ-, κλ-, πλ-

- for example: γρ-, θρ-, κρ-, πρ-, τρ-, χρ-

- for example: θμ-, σμ-, γν-, πν-

➢ ACCENT

Biblical Greek has a formal system of accents that point out *stressed,* or *accented,* syllables. Gaining a working knowledge of accents will make reading and studying Biblical Greek easier. In some cases your knowledge of accents will help you distinguish between otherwise identical present and future verbal "tense"-forms. A detailed discussion of all the rules associated with accents is beyond our scope here. We focus, however, on a few basic thoughts.

- names of accents

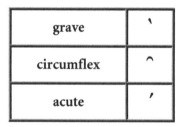

grave	`
circumflex	^
acute	´

Figure 6: Accent Names

---

[9] Some phoneticians refer to λ and ρ as LIQUIDS. These two consonants share a common feature of involving both the tip of the tongue and the alveolar ridge for their sound production.

- accents and vowel quantity/length

  Vowel quantity or length affects the type of accent you may find in a syllable. The GRAVE and ACUTE accents may be found on either long or short vowels. You will find the CIRCUMFLEX accent only over long vowels.

grave	long or short
circumflex	long
acute	long or short

Figure 7: Vowel Quantity Associated with Accents

- syllable position

  Accents are a factor *only with the last three syllables of a word.* They thus occur only in the antepenult, penult, and ultima syllables. The ACUTE accent may occur in all three. The CIRCUMFLEX occurs in the last two, while the GRAVE is only in the ultima.

Here is a chart that puts these concepts together.

		Syllable Position		
Accent Name	Vowel Quantity	Antepenult	Penult	Ultima
grave	long or short			`
circumflex	long		^	^
acute	long or short	´	´	´

Figure 8: Overview of Accents Associated with Syllables

TRANSLATION

What is happening when two people talk or write? They are, in part, encoding and decoding a code—they're encoding and decoding meaning conveyed in forms that are particular to a language. This is likely not the answer you readily had in mind, but let us explore this.

Language includes at least two concepts:

➢ FORM, or to be more linguistically technical, CODE, and

➢ MEANING.

A code alone does not communicate. An unknown language can sound or look like a jumble of nothing—remember what a page of Biblical Greek first looked like to you! Every language has its own specific system for linking its code, that is, linking its form, with meaning. A spoken and written language has a

➢ PHONOLOGY, a system of sounds (if the language is written, these sounds are connected with a writing system);

➢ LEXICON, that is, a vocabulary;

➢ GRAMMAR, a set of patterns for making meaningful expressions.

MEANING is universal. Though different cultures may organize and conceive things differently, we share many things. For example, many cultures express casual greetings. In the morning, those who speak English may convey the greetings as "Good morning." "Good morning" is the FORM English speakers use to convey a *meaning*ful greeting. Form is the unique pattern of a specific language.

Each language has its own distinctive form, and the same meaning may be expressed in another language in quite a different form. "Good morning" is an adjective preceding a common noun. A Modern Hebrew speaker might say *boqer tov* (literally: "morning good"), a grammatically masculine and singular common noun followed by a grammatically masculine singular adjective. In Nigeria, in Hausa, one might say *Ina kwana?* "How's sleep?" Again, form is the unique pattern of a specific language.

We have been talking about the word *mean(ing)*; let us use it to illustrate something. Consider the following expressions.

1. That was no mean (**insignificant**) accomplishment.

2. They are so mean (**cruel**) to me.

3. This will mean (**result in**) the end of our regime.

4. This means so much (**is so important**) to me.

5. I mean (**intend**) to help if I can.

6. Keep off the grass! This means (**refers to**) you.

7. Those clouds mean (**are a sign of**) rain.

8. She doesn't mean (**believe**) what she said.

These expressions illustrate that one form or pattern, in this case the letters M-E-A-N, can express different meanings. When an English speaker infuses different morphemes and lexemes (see definitions, p. 4) into the one form M-E-A-N, this one form (M-E-A-N) can encode different meanings.

Now, consider the following expressions.

1. Is this seat taken?

2. May I sit here?

3. Is this seat empty?

These are three different forms to express one meaning, namely, to express the intent of a person wanting to sit. Different forms may thus express one similar, if not identical, meaning.

In working with languages, you will quickly discover that expressions that retain similar form may actually express very different meanings. Consider the English expression "His heart is cold," which can mean "He is unfeeling." When transferred word for word, literally, into Mambila (a language in Nigeria), the meaning becomes in that language "He is peaceful." When the same is done into

Cinyanja (a language in Zambia), the meaning is "He is afraid."[10] I hope you see a problem here. Very different meanings might arise for an expression transferred word for word into another language.

The starting point of translation is the SOURCE LANGUAGE (SL). A translation should attempt to express the SL *meaning* into a TARGET LANGUAGE (TL).

By now you have seen that *form* in each language is unique. Thus, translation must entail a change in form. This change in form does not matter provided that the *meaning* of the message is unchanged, or changed as little as possible.

Translation is not simply a process of only taking SL words or phrases and transferring them into similar TL words and phrases:

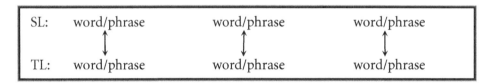

This is known as a GLOSS among translators. It is not the same as a translation.

The translation task, rather, is one of understanding the forms of the SL and distilling the meaning from the SL vocabulary and grammar and expressing this meaning into TL forms that convey the equivalent SL meaning. You must discover the meaning of the source language—in this case, Biblical Greek—and convey this meaning through the appropriate form of the target language:

---

[10] Examples come from Katharine Barnwell, *Introduction to Semantics and Translation* (2d ed.; Horsley Green, England: Summer Institute of Linguistics, 1980), 12.

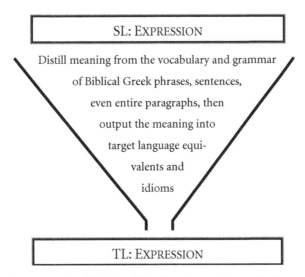

SL: EXPRESSION

Distill meaning from the vocabulary and grammar
of Biblical Greek phrases, sentences,
even entire paragraphs, then
output the meaning into
target language equi-
valents and
idioms

TL: EXPRESSION

At times the stakes are quite high in this glossing and translating process. When Jerome decided to continue the Old Latin's use of *iustifico* (a legal term) for δικαιόω (a legal and ethical term), he was limiting the meaning of the word more than the source language (Biblical Greek) limited it. The confusion continued on through Melanchthon (see the fourth article of his *Apology for the Augsburg Confession)* into the twentieth century. Only now is it beginning to be resolved with the recently released *Joint Declaration on the Doctrine of Justification,* which the Roman Catholic and Lutheran churches have issued.[11]

TRANSLATIONS

Since language includes both form and meaning, we are able to characterize translations according to how form-oriented or meaning-oriented they are. We can view source and target languages on a form–meaning continuum.

FORM-ORIENTED translations try to follow the form of the SL and are known as *literal.*

MEANING-ORIENTED ones are known as *idiomatic* or *dynamic equivalent.*

---

[11] I thank Mark Reasoner for this example.

Here is a continuum for characterizing some English translations. I have added an illustrative phrase from 1 Corinthians 16:20.

FORM   MEANING

COMPLETELY LITERAL	MODIFIED LITERAL		IDIOMATIC		
Interlinear	KJV	NRSV	NIV	GNB	CEV
	NASB		NAB	NJB	
"kiss holy"	"holy kiss"		"hearty hug"		
			"warm handshake"		

COMPLETELY LITERAL. An interlinear is completely literal, completely form-oriented. Its value lies in showing the exegete the precise word order and other forms of the SL. Here is a completely literal presentation of 1 Corinthians 11:10:

> "Because-of this ought the woman authority have on the head because-of the angels."

MODIFIED LITERAL. These translations modify the form of the SL just to the extent that sentence structure is acceptable in the TL. Individual words, however, tend to be translated literally. The result is that though sentence structure is correct, the translation may not sound natural to a speaker of the contemporary language. Further, it may not say enough to bring clarity to the reader. This, admittedly, is a mixed bag of good and bad. Here is a modified literal translation of 1 Corinthians 11:10:

> "Therefore the woman ought to have authority on her head because of the angels."

Here sentence structure follows normal English expectations, and in this case, it does not sound unnatural. The verse, however, contains some ambiguity. Does the writer refer to *women* or *wives*? Does the writer envision that the "woman" ought to have someone or something else be an authority over her? Or does this verse say that the woman ought to have authority on her *own* head?

The value of a modified literal translation can be that it does not go far "beyond" the SL. But that can cut two ways. The translation does not give much more than the SL, but it may also not give enough to bring clarity. Here is where *idiomatic* translations can be helpful as well as perilous. To those we now turn.

IDIOMATIC. These translations strive to use natural forms—grammatical constructions and words—of the TL to convey the meaning of the SL. A truly idiomatic translation will sound as if it were written originally in the TL; it will not sound like a translation. This is the goal of most Bible translators entrusted today with the task of providing Scriptures to groups who still do not have a translation of the Bible. Here are a couple of idiomatic translations of 1 Corinthians 11:10:

> "On account of the angels, then, a woman should have a covering over her head to show that she is under her husband's authority." (GNB = Good News Bible)

> "And so, because of this, and also because of the angels, a woman ought to wear something on her head, as a sign of her authority." (CEV = Contemporary English Version)

The *value* of seeing these two translations is that we can see their attempt to bring clarity to a rather ambiguous verse. GNB understands "woman" to be a wife (because it uses "husband"), and it makes clear that a wife is to be under her husband's authority. CEV, while not committing to "woman" versus "wife," conveys that a woman has her *own* authority. She has within *herself* the right to behave as she sees fit. She just ought to wear something as a sign of this.

The *peril*, as you now likely see, is that these two meaning-oriented translations convey two very different meanings. I have chosen an extreme case to highlight a peril. Being aware of the peril, though, allows one to be able to embrace cautiously the great value of meaning-oriented translations. They are attempting to bring *meaning* more clearly to the reader.

I generally recommend to my students, when they wish to consult a translation, a strategy of reading a variety of translations from the entire form–meaning spectrum.

TRANSLATING HOMEWORK IN FIRST-YEAR BIBLICAL GREEK COURSES

As you begin trying to express Biblical Greek into English, you will likely be very form-oriented. This, at first, is not a bad idea. It allows your instructor to see that you are understanding the Greek form and patterns. As the year continues, though, and as you gain confidence in the language, strive for a meaning-oriented translation.

Part II
Building Blocks

DECLENSION

The form of words can change. This is known as INFLECTION. Notice, for example, a couple of ways that English can inflect to show plurality. *Student* becomes *students*. The concept of plurality—or to be more linguistically precise, the morpheme of 'plurality'—is conveyed in this word through adding an *-s*. *Woman,* on the other hand, becomes *women*. Changing an internal vowel conveys plurality in this particular word.

An inflectional pattern is called a DECLENSION. This word is especially at home in the study of Biblical Greek, where nouns are grouped into three basic declensions. Through the course of your learning, you will become acquainted with the characteristics of each declension in Biblical Greek. For example, Biblical Greek nouns that end in *alpha* or *eta* are placed in the first declension and are mostly feminine in gender (see GENDER, p. 30), for example, γραφή *writing, Scripture.*

GENDER

GENDER in language refers to classifying words usually as MASCULINE, FEMININE, or NEUTER. It plays an important structural role in many languages but not in English. Nouns and verbs in English have no special markings (morphs) for gender. In Biblical Greek, gender is important and plays a role in most nominals (specifically, nouns/substantives, pronouns, adjectives, and participles).

ENGLISH

Though English nouns and verbs have no special markings for gender, *nouns* typically reflect their biological sex, where it is clear. Male entities are *masculine*. Female entities are *feminine*. Other things tend to be *neuter*. When we replace a noun with a pronoun, we assign it gender.

➢ We use masculine pronouns to replace nouns that refer to males.

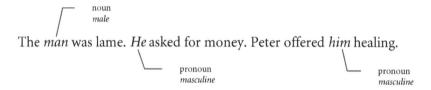

The *man* was lame. *He* asked for money. Peter offered *him* healing.

➢ We use feminine pronouns to replace nouns that refer to females.

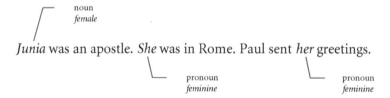

Junia was an apostle. *She* was in Rome. Paul sent *her* greetings.

➢ We commonly, but not always, use the neuter pronoun *it* to replace all other nouns.

Herod built the *temple*. People worshiped at *it*.

30

But notice exceptions:

The great *ocean liner* left port. *She* was grand.

BIBLICAL GREEK

Most nominals (specifically, nouns/substantives, pronouns, adjectives, and participles) in Biblical Greek are *masculine, feminine,* or *neuter.* Biblical Greek does, sometimes, match gender according to biological sex. On the whole, though, gender is a *grammatical* phenomenon referring to the groupings in which most nominals find themselves.

We find some general patterns relating to gender. The majority of Biblical Greek nouns in the first declension are feminine; the majority found in the second declension are masculine. *Trees, islands, countries,* and many *abstract* nouns tend to be feminine. *Rivers* tend to be masculine.

31

NUMBER

NUMBER, as a grammatical concept, refers to the quantity of participants a word denotes. When a word denotes only *one* participant, we call it SINGULAR. When a word refers to more than one participant, the word is PLURAL.

➤ Nouns that allow us to enumerate the number of participants are known as COUNTABLE NOUNS.

➤ Nouns that are singular in form yet refer to a group are COLLECTIVE NOUNS.

➤ Verbs convey number, usually agreeing with the number of the grammatical subject of the clause.

ENGLISH

We form the plural of countable nouns in a variety of ways.

➤ add the sound [-s], often written as *-s*, or add the sound [-əz] after a sibilant, often written as *-es*, to a singular noun

    path   path*s*

    kiss   kiss*es*

➤ more substantial changes

    man   m*e*n

    child   child*ren*

    mouse   m*ice*   (but if referring to a computer mouse, commonly mouse*s*)

➤ no change

    sheep   sheep

Collective nouns are singular in form yet refer to a group. American and British English speakers treat collective nouns differently. Americans generally use a verb that is singular whereas the British commonly use one that is plural.

➤ American English

The *team is* winning.

➤ British English

The *team are* winning.

BIBLICAL GREEK

Biblical Greek nouns convey singular and plural. Distinguishing between singular and plural entails identifying the endings associated with the case (see CASE, p. 34) and the declension (see DECLENSION, p. 29) of the noun. (See EXCURSUS: THE ORDER OF CASE IN PARADIGMS, p. 37, for the logic behind the order of cases in this textbook's charts.)

		1st/2d Declension			3d Declension	
		masculine	feminine	neuter	masc/fem	neuter
Singular	nom	ς, λόγος	-, γραφή	ν, ἔργον	ς, σάρξ[12]	-, ὄνομα
	acc	ν, λόγον	ν, γραφήν	ν, ἔργον	α/ν, σάρκα	-, ὄνομα
	gen	υ, λόγου	ς, γραφῆς	υ, ἔργου	ος, σαρκός	ος, ὀνόματος
	dat	ι, λόγῳ[13]	ι, γραφῇ	ι, ἔργῳ	ι, σαρκί	ι, ὀνόματι
Plural	nom	ι, λόγοι	ι, γραφαί	α, ἔργα	ες, σάρκες	α, ὀνόματα
	acc	υς, λόγους	ς, γραφάς	α, ἔργα	ας, σάρκας	α, ὀνόματα
	gen	ων, λόγων	ων, γραφῶν	ων, ἔργων	ων, σαρκῶν	ων, ὀνομάτων
	dat	ις, λόγοις	ις, γραφαῖς	ις, ἔργοις	σι[14], σαρξί	σι[15], ὀνόμασι

Figure 9: Singular and Plural Endings of Biblical Greek Nouns

Most of Biblical Greek's verbal forms convey singular and plural.

---

[12] This form develops from σαρκ + ς (/κ/ + /ς/ > /ξ/).

[13] The *iota* is subscript.

[14] Or σι(ν) with movable *nu.*

[15] Or σι(ν) with movable *nu.*

CASE

CASE is a system of marking nominals (nouns, pronouns, adjectives, participles, etc.) to express syntactic or structural relationships.

Going into more depth, we can see that case, as a system in general, expresses a relationship that dependent nominals have with their HEAD.[16] In a verbal clause, for example, we can understand that a verb is the most *prominent* head because it is largely responsible for which dependent nominals may be present within the clause. In Biblical Greek the verb δίδωμι *give*, for instance, may be the head of the following dependent nominals:

(1) a *giver* (perhaps expressed as a separate subject in the *nominative case*),

(2) a *gift* (expressed by a direct object in the *accusative case*), and

(3) a *recipient* (expressed by an indirect object in the *dative case*).

The verb could have other dependents that express time or location in a choice of cases. Deep within that overall clausal structure, a preposition, such as διά, while dependent on the verb, may itself function as a head of a dependent nominal that follows (in the accusative or genitive case). A pronoun, particularly in the *genitive case* and where it expresses possession, such as αὐτοῦ *of him* is dependent on a head nominal, such as οἱ μαθηταί, for example, οἱ μαθηταί αὐτοῦ *his disciples*. (οἱ μαθηταί, in turn, could be dependent on a head elsewhere in the clause, particularly if it is in a case that is not the nominative.)

ENGLISH

English has very little of a case system. Common nouns routinely have a (1) NORMAL or COMMON or NONPOSSESSIVE CASE (*The **vessel** was full; She filled the **vessel***) and a (2) POSSESSIVE CASE (*He spilled the **vessel's** contents*). Our *pronouns* show us the most prominent use of case, having a SUBJECT CASE, OBJECT

---

[16] This discussion is largely dependent on Barry J. Blake, *Case* (2d ed.; Cambridge Textbooks in Linguistics; Cambridge: Cambridge University Press, 2001), 1–17.

CASE (object of verb or preposition), and **POSSESSIVE CASE**. We shall use them to illustrate case in English.

SUBJECT CASE

We can use pronouns, such as personal and relative, as, for example, the subject of a verb (see the chapter on **PRONOUN**, p. 121 and **SUBJECT**, p. 198) or as a **PREDICATE NOMINATIVE**, which is any nominal—not just a pronoun—in the *predicate* of a clause where the verb is *be* or *become* and where that nominal refers to the subject.

Personal Pronoun

I talked, and *you* listened.

> *Who* talked? *I* = subject
>
> *I* is the subject of the verb *talked*
>
> *Who* listened? *you* = subject
>
> *you* is the subject of *listened*

Relative Pronoun

The woman *who* touched you is healed.

> The relative pronoun *who* is the subject within the relative clause ***who touched you***

Predicate Nominative

It is *he*.

> *he* is within the predicate *is he*
>
> The predicate has the verb *be*
>
> *he* refers to the subject *It*
>
> *he* is a predicate nominative

OBJECT CASE

Pronouns, such as personal and relative, can be used as, for example, the object of a verb or the object of a preposition.

Personal Pronoun

Herod saw *him* but spoke to *us*.

> Herod saw *whom? him* = object of verb
>
> *him* is the object of the verb *saw*
>
> Herod spoke *to whom? us* = object of preposition
>
> *us* is the object of the preposition *to*

Relative Pronoun

The woman *whom* you touched is healed.

> The relative pronoun *whom* is the object of the verb *touch* within the
> relative clause **whom** *you touched* (*you* is the subject)

POSSESSIVE CASE

Possessive pronouns are examples of the possessive case. They specify the *possessor* of a replaced noun.

> Herodias and Herod had different desires. *Hers* was for revenge. *His* was to
> keep a promise.
>
> > The replaced noun is *desires*

BIBLICAL GREEK

Unlike English, Biblical Greek has a vibrant case system—five cases (be aware,
though, that you might encounter talk of eight).[17] Biblical Greek offers five distinct forms that we identify as case. In the order of the number of their occurrences in Biblical Greek, the cases are

nominative,
accusative,
genitive,
dative,
vocative.

---

[17] The other three are the ablative, locative, and instrumental.

In Biblical Greek, the morpheme (see the definition, p. 4) of 'case' does not bundle itself *alone* to a nominal, as it does, for example, in Turkish. Case in Biblical Greek, rather, fuses with 'number' (see the chapter NUMBER, p. 32); one accounts for case *and* number in the case endings. For example, –ος, as an ending, conveys *nominative* case, *singular* number. We can add to this the concept of 'gender' (see the chapter GENDER, p. 30), which also plays a role in the overall form of the nominal.

EXCURSUS: THE ORDER OF CASE IN PARADIGMS

I have arranged case in the paradigms of this book in the order of

nominative,
accusative,
genitive, and
dative.

Many teaching grammars place the accusative at the end, after genitive and dative. Languages, however, seem to show a CASE HIERARCHY; that is, cases tend to be built up in a particular order. The order is, according to Barry Blake,

nominative,
accusative,
genitive,
dative,
locative,
ablative/instrumental,
etc.[18]

If a language has, for example, a dative case, it more than likely has a genitive, an accusative, and a nominative. In the other direction, the language might or might not have a locative or an ablative/instrumental. If it has a genitive, it more than likely has an accusative and nominative, but it might not have a dative, locative, and so forth.

---

[18] Blake, *Case*, 89, 155–160.

The paradigms throughout this book reflect the case hierarchy for Biblical Greek. The nominative case is the most common, followed by the accusative, genitive, then dative. With roughly 300 occurrences of the vocative (compared with around 24,600 for the nominative), the vocative does not make its way onto the paradigms. In laying out the paradigms, I felt it was advantageous to follow not only more universal linguistic data but Biblical Greek's own statistics.

NOMINATIVE CASE

Defining the **NOMINATIVE CASE** is a challenging task. The Greeks give us helpful insight into their thinking process. They called it ἡ ὀνομαστικὴ πτῶσις *the naming case*. It *explicitly* could "name" an entity responsible for some verbal process (over and above the *person* and *number* already wrapped up in a finite verb's form), usually what we call a *subject*. It is a case that is also used for syntactic elements—entire clauses, in fact—that are to be isolated from other syntactic elements.

The nominative case, when we consider its variety of functions (not just the one that identifies a subject), appears to *denote an entity* more so than to express the relationship between an entity and a verbal process. In a verbal clause, for example, the nominative, if used, *denotes* or, to be Greek about it, *names* a syntactic entity. The accusative and dative, if used, express *relationships* around the verbal process as they relate to the *named*, or nominative entity. An entire clause itself, however, can stand within another clause and be in the nominative case. Here is where the nominative more clearly shows its work of *denoting* an entity than of expressing a relationship.

In Biblical Greek a clause with verbal or verbless predication has a subject and a predicate. We shall keep this in mind as we look now at some of the more principal functions of the nominative case. Here is an illustration of these functions.

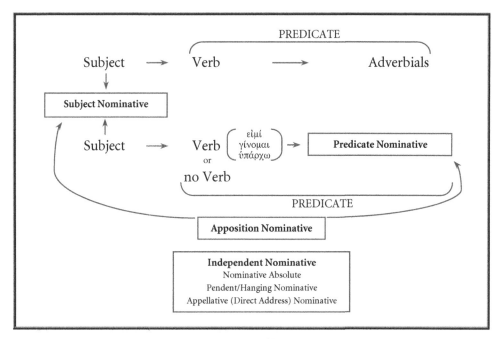

Figure 10: Select Functions of the Nominative

Subject Nominative

The most common function of the nominative case is to denote the syntactic subject of a finite verb.

ὁ πατὴρ ἔχει ζωὴν	*The father* has life.
the father he-has life	John 5:26

Predicate Nominative

One environment for the predicate nominative is a *verbal* clause where the verbal process is RELATIONAL or one of BEING (see the section RELATIONAL = BEING, p. 205 in the chapter SEMANTICS: PROCESSES, ROLES, AND CIRCUMSTANCES). The verbal process is most commonly conveyed through εἰμί *be, exist*, γίνομαι *become*, and ὑπάρχω *be, be at one's disposal*. The PREDICATE in this structure is frequently relationally linked to the subject, often *descriptively* (= conveying an attribute) or *equatively* (= *equal*), and it shares the subject's nominative case. This is a predicate nominative—the *predicate* is in the *nominative case*.

39

ἡ   δὲ   γυνὴ   ἦν   Ἑλληνίς
the now woman she-was **Gentile**

Now the woman was *a Gentile.*

Mark 7:26

The other environment for a predicate nominative is a *verbless* clause where two or more nominative elements are juxtaposed, routinely expressing a *relation* of BEING, whether *descriptive* or *equative.*

πνεῦμα ὁ   θεός
spirit   (the) God

God is *spirit.*

John 4:24

All this talk of subjects and predicate nominatives both being in the nominative case understandably leads to a question: How do you know which is which? Why, for instance, did I say, in the last example, that ὁ θεός was the subject and not the predicate nominative?

A principle lies behind the choice for a syntactic/grammatical subject. The element that appears to be ***more specific, more specified*** tends to be identified as a subject. This still does not make the choice clear at times, but it appears to be a good rule of thumb. In practice, this principle plays out in the following fashion.

> ➤ **Pronoun:** if one grammatical element is a pronoun (personal, demonstrative, etc.), treat it as the subject. If both elements are pronominal, treat the first one as the subject (the logic here is that "front ends" of clauses are where we often expect to find the more prominent grammatical elements).

ἐγὼ γάρ εἰμι πρεσβύτης
I   for   I-am **old-man**

I, indeed, am *an old man.*

Luke 1:18

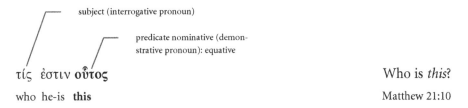

τίς ἐστιν **οὗτος**

who he-is **this**

Who is *this?*

Matthew 21:10

➢ **Proper Noun/Name:** if one grammatical element is a proper noun, treat it as the subject. If both elements are proper nouns, treat the first one as the subject.

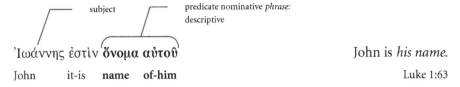

Ἰωάννης ἐστὶν **ὄνομα αὐτοῦ**

John   it-is   **name   of-him**

John is *his name.*

Luke 1:63

➢ **Arthrous/Articular Noun:** if one grammatical element is articular (having an article), treat it as the subject. If both elements are articular, treat the first one as the subject.

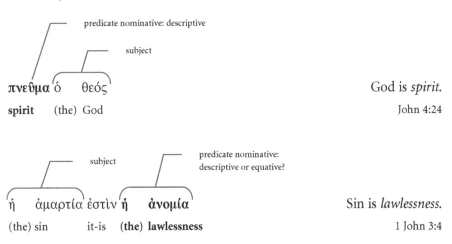

πνεῦμα ὁ   θεός

spirit   (the) God

God is *spirit.*

John 4:24

ἡ   ἁμαρτία ἐστὶν ἡ   **ἀνομία**

(the) sin   it-is   **(the) lawlessness**

Sin is *lawlessness.*

1 John 3:4

➢ **Anarthrous Nouns:** if both grammatical elements are anarthrous nouns (*not* having an article), treat the first one as the subject.

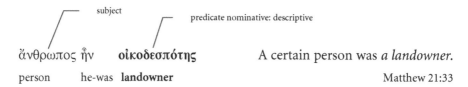

ἄνθρωπος ἦν	**οἰκοδεσπότης**	A certain person was *a landowner.*
person	he-was **landowner**	Matthew 21:33

Apposition Nominative

Apposition refers to the (1) juxtaposition, that is, routinely, the simple side-by-sideness of a nominal (or nominal phrase) to another nominal (or nominal phrase), (2) where both refer to the same entity (3) while being in the *same* syntactic slot within a clause. In the case of *nominative* apposition, two nominals (or nominal phrases) sit side by side, both in the nominative case, both referring to the same entity, and both residing in the same syntactic slot in the clause. The first nominal in the nominative case may have any of that case's functions (for example, subject, predicate nominative, etc.). The following or juxtaposed or *appositive* nominative says something more about the first nominative.

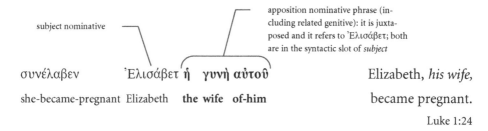

συνέλαβεν	Ἐλισάβετ **ἡ γυνὴ αὐτοῦ**	Elizabeth, *his wife,*
she-became-pregnant	Elizabeth **the wife of-him**	became pregnant.
		Luke 1:24

Independent Nominative

The nominative has several functions grouped here under the term *independent.* These functions share the trait of, shall we say, *"unlinkedness"* with the text around them. More explicitly, they lack *formal grammatical agreement* with the surrounding text. In a certain sense, we can think of them as *interjectional.* They are insert-like: a title, prominent information for highlighting, or a calling out to someone. Earlier I said that the nominative case appears to *denote an entity* more so than to express a relationship. We see this particularly in these so-called independent nominatives. We shall look at the NOMINATIVE ABSOLUTE, PEN-

42

DENT/HANGING NOMINATIVE, and the APPELLATIVE (DIRECT ADDRESS) NOMINATIVE.

Nominative Absolute

According to many of Biblical Greek's grammarians, the nominative absolute is a type of introductory or salutatory interjection into the text, residing outside a clause (therefore, syntactically unhooked) and itself *not* being a clause (it does *not* involve predication). Within the nominative absolute construction, one will, of course, find other cases to identify the relationships within the construction.

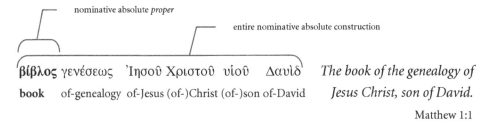

βίβλος γενέσεως Ἰησοῦ Χριστοῦ υἱοῦ Δαυὶδ *The book of the genealogy of*
book of-genealogy of-Jesus (of-)Christ (of-)son of-David *Jesus Christ, son of David.*

Matthew 1:1

Pendent/Hanging Nominative

Similar to the nominative absolute, the pendent/hanging nominative also resides outside other clause structures. Although it lacks *formal grammatical* agreement with an associated clause, it has an *explicit referential* link with it. The prominent entity in the pendent/hanging construction is referenced in an associated clause. This explicit referential link is what separates the pendent/hanging nominative from the nominative absolute, which does *not* have a grammatical or explicit referential link. The pendent/hanging nominative is a way for the language to highlight particularly important or prominent information, something linguists call FOCUS (see FOCUS/FOCALITY, p. 217).

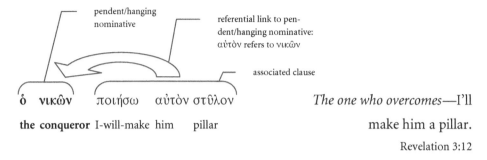

ὁ νικῶν   ποιήσω   αὐτὸν στῦλον

the conqueror I-will-make him   pillar

The one who overcomes—I'll

make him a pillar.

Revelation 3:12

Appellative (Direct Address) Nominative

The nominative is used in direct address, referring to an addressee. This is commonly the function of the vocative case.

ἡ παῖς, ἔγειρε

the child, arise

Child, arise!

Luke 8:54

ACCUSATIVE CASE

Primarily related to the verbal process expressed in a clause, the accusative case describes the verbal process's *extent* or *limitation.*

In Biblical Greek a clause with verbal predication commonly has a subject and always a predicate. The predicate has a verb and may have ADVERBIALS.

Some linguists distinguish between adverbials that are *complements* (in a sense of "*complete*-ment") and those that are *adjuncts.* The former refers to a *necessary* constituent (one needed for completeness), the latter, an *unnecessary* or *optional* one.[19]

Dividing adverbials into two main categories is helpful: (1) ADVERBIAL COMPLE-MENT and (2) ADVERBIAL ADJUNCT, often called the ADVERBIAL MODIFIER. One particular adverbial complement that involves the accusative case is the COMPLE-MENT ACCUSATIVE. One particular adverbial adjunct subcategory that involves the accusative is the ADVERBIAL ADJUNCT ACCUSATIVE. The *complement accusative*

---

[19] John Lyons, *Introduction to Theoretical Linguistics* (Cambridge: Cambridge University Press, 1968), 43–50.

is so called because of its necessity when it occurs. The *adverbial adjunct accusative* has in mind accusative elements that are adjuncts. Under *complement accusative* and *adverbial adjunct accusative* we find the bulk of the accusative's roles.

Where the verbal processes take the form of an infinitive, however, the accusative case often marks the *subject* role of that verbal process. This is the SUBJECT ACCUSATIVE function.

The accusative may also be in *apposition* to any other accusative in the functions we have just encountered: APPOSITION ACCUSATIVE.

We also encounter, as in the nominative, an INDEPENDENT ACCUSATIVE (one of which we shall discuss is the PENDENT/HANGING ACCUSATIVE).

Here is an illustration of the accusative's functions.

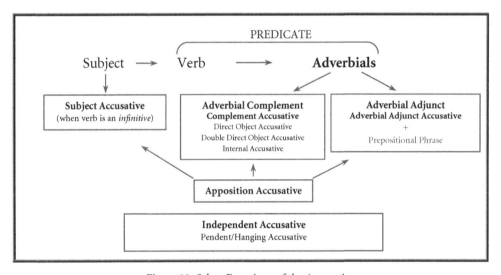

Figure 11: Select Functions of the Accusative

Later, under DATIVE CASE (p. 54), we shall add the roles of that case to our notion of *adverbials*. For now, we focus on the accusative.

Adverbial Complement

Complement Accusative

Verbs can govern **OBJECTS**. The objects are *complements;* that is, when they occur, they *complete* the verbal process. They are necessary, needed for wholeness.

Syntactically, we call them objects. *Semantically,* they can stand in a variety of roles related to the verbal process: for example, **MATERIAL** = **DOING** ("Herod *killed the boys*"); **MENTAL** = **SENSING** ("He *heard the cries*"). (See the discussion under **SEMANTICS: PROCESSES, ROLES, AND CIRCUMSTANCES**, p. 203.)

We shall consider three types of complement accusatives: (1) direct object accusative, (2) double direct object accusative, and (3) internal accusative.

Direct Object Accusative

A direct object accusative receives a verbal process. A verb that governs a direct object is known as a *transitive* verb (think of the verb as the "rapid *transit*" system for conveying the verbal process to a direct object).

ἐδίδασκεν	τοὺς ὄχλους	He was teaching *the crowds.*
he-was-teaching	**the** **crowds**	Luke 5:3

Double Direct Object Accusative

Some verbs are doubly transitive; they take two direct objects. Verbal processes that include the notion of 'cause/causation' often take two direct objects ("make *him* [object₁] eat *fish* [object₂]"), as do verbs that convey the notions of 'speaking' (*ask, answer, say, command, teach,* etc.) and 'giving/receiving' (*give, offer, receive,* etc.).

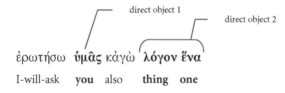

ἐρωτήσω	ὑμᾶς κἀγὼ	λόγον ἕνα	I will also ask *you one thing.*
I-will-ask	**you** also	**thing** one	Matthew 21:24

Internal Accusative

An internal accusative expresses the verb's process. "Fight *the fight*" is an example. The internal accusative shares the root of the verb or has another *close* semantic link with the verb's meaning. Although in many instances the internal accusative functions as the direct object, sometimes the internal accusative, instead of being the direct object, makes a comment about the verb's action. We shall see in time that making a comment about a verbal process is what the *adverbial adjunct accusative* routinely does. The sharing of a *root* or other *close* semantic link between an internal accusative and its head verb places this accusative within the sphere of a *complement* rather than an *adverbial adjunct accusative*.

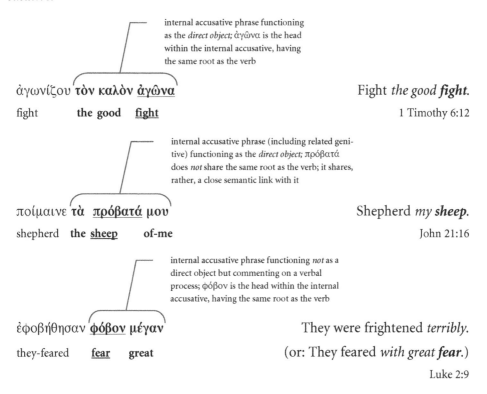

internal accusative phrase functioning as the *direct object;* ἀγῶνα is the head within the internal accusative, having the same root as the verb

ἀγωνίζου **τὸν καλὸν** <u>ἀγῶνα</u>

fight **the good** <u>fight</u>

Fight *the good* **fight**.

1 Timothy 6:12

internal accusative phrase (including related genitive) functioning as the *direct object;* πρόβατά does *not* share the same root as the verb; it shares, rather, a close semantic link with it

ποίμαινε **τὰ** **πρόβατά** μου

shepherd **the** <u>sheep</u> of-me

Shepherd *my* **sheep**.

John 21:16

internal accusative phrase functioning *not* as a direct object but commenting on a verbal process; φόβον is the head within the internal accusative, having the same root as the verb

ἐφοβήθησαν **φόβον** μέγαν

they-feared <u>**fear**</u> great

They were frightened *terribly*.

(or: They feared *with great* **fear**.)

Luke 2:9

This last example is worth a longer look. Understand that φόβον μέγαν is making a comment *about* the verbal process of *fearing*. φόβον μέγαν could be a direct object *if* the writer meant to say that people were afraid of fear—they feared *fear*.

47

They often were fearful, for example, and are now afraid of the fear that takes hold of them. This meaning, however, is not what the writer intends (understood from the context)—they are filled *with* fear.

Adverbial Adjunct

With the idea of *complement* and *adjunct* in mind, adverbial adjuncts are indirectly governed by verbs, and they refer to *circumstances* associated with the verbal process. The dative case and prepositional phrases play a large role as adverbial adjuncts in addition to the *adverbial adjunct accusative.*

Adverbial Adjunct Accusative

The adverbial adjunct accusative conveys the *circumstances* associated with a verbal process. They commonly describe such circumstances as these:

➤ manner

ἄρα	Χριστὸς	**δωρεὰν**	ἀπέθανεν	Then Christ died *for no reason.*
then	Christ	**without-cause**	he-died	Galatians 2:21

➤ space/place/location

ἐληλακότες	οὖν	ὡς	**σταδίους εἴκοσι πέντε**	Thus they rowed
they-rowed	thus	about	**stades twenty five**	about *twenty-five stades.*
				John 6:19

➤ time

τί	ὧδε	ἑστήκατε	**ὅλην τὴν ἡμέραν**	ἀργοί	Why have you stood here
why	here	you-have-stood	**all the day**	idle	idle *the whole day?*
					Matthew 20:6

Subject Accusative

Not uncommonly the subject role of an infinitive is in the accusative case. In many instances, the infinitive's subject is in the accusative because of its function in the clause. This is parallel with English:

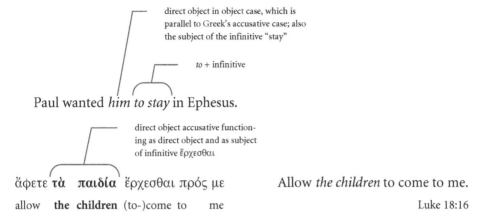

Paul wanted *him to stay* in Ephesus.

ἄφετε **τὰ παιδία** ἔρχεσθαι πρός με

allow **the children** (to-)come to me

Allow *the children* to come to me.

Luke 18:16

In Biblical Greek, though, the subject, *even when it should **not** be accusative because of its role in a clause,* may be in the accusative when governing an infinitive.

Apposition Accusative

My discussion under **APPOSITION NOMINATIVE**, p. 42, defined *apposition*. In the case of an *accusative* in apposition, similarly to a nominative in apposition, two nominals (or nominal phrases) sit side by side, both in the accusative case, both referring to the same entity, and both residing in the same syntactic slot in the clause. The first nominal in the accusative case may have any of that case's functions (for example, direct object accusative, internal accusative, adverbial adjunct accusative, etc.). The following or juxtaposed or *appositive* accusative says something more about the first accusative.

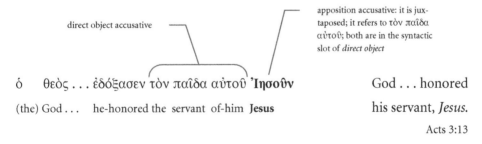

ὁ θεὸς ... ἐδόξασεν τὸν παῖδα αὐτοῦ ᾽Ιησοῦν

(the) God ... he-honored the servant of-him **Jesus**

God ... honored

his servant, *Jesus.*

Acts 3:13

Independent Accusative

The functions of the independent accusative, like the independent nominative, *lack formal grammatical agreement* with the surrounding text. We shall look at one such function: the PENDENT/HANGING ACCUSATIVE.

Pendent/Hanging Accusative

Although the pendent/hanging accusative *lacks* formal grammatical agreement with an associated clause, it has an *explicit referential* link with it. The prominent entity in the pendent/hanging construction is referenced in an associated clause. We have something similar in English: "Me?—I'm planning to go." *Me* is in the object case and is referenced by *I* in the associated clause. The pendent/hanging accusative is a way for the language to highlight particularly important or prominent information, something linguists call FOCUS (see FOCUS/FOCALITY, p. 217).

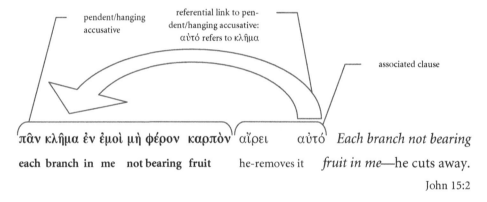

| pendent/hanging accusative | referential link to pendent/hanging accusative: αὐτό refers to κλῆμα | associated clause |

πᾶν κλῆμα ἐν ἐμοὶ μὴ φέρον καρπὸν αἴρει αὐτό *Each branch not bearing*

each branch in me not bearing fruit he-removes it *fruit in me*—he cuts away.

John 15:2

GENITIVE CASE

The genitive case, similar to the accusative, is a case that *limits* or *restricts*. But whereas the accusative and, as we shall see, the dative, are primarily *ad-verbial* (linked "*to the verb*"), the genitive is primarily *ad-nominal* (linked "*to the nominal/noun*"). The genitive is most often the case of a nominal that is governed by another nominal.

The study of the genitive is encumbered by what seem to be, at first blush, as many different functions as occurrences. We shall limit ourselves to highlighting

four major functions: **SUBJECT GENITIVE, ADVERBIAL GENITIVE, ADJECTIVE GENI-
TIVE,** and **VERB-GOVERNED GENITIVE.** Under each, reference grammars may have
a host of semantically driven subcategories.

Subject Genitive

A genitive may have an underlying *subject* role when the head or governing
nominal suggests a verbal process. It may be the agent/"do–er" of the verbal
process or have other subject-like roles.

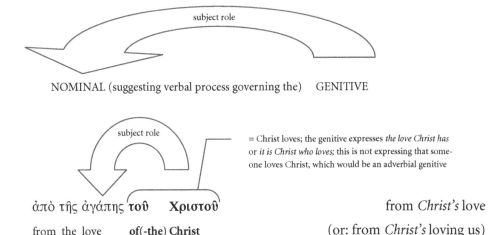

NOMINAL (suggesting verbal process governing the)   GENITIVE

= Christ loves; the genitive expresses *the love Christ has*
or *it is Christ who loves;* this is not expressing that someone loves Christ, which would be an adverbial genitive

ἀπὸ τῆς ἀγάπης **τοῦ   Χριστοῦ**

from the love   **of(-the) Christ**

from *Christ's* love

(or: from *Christ's* loving us)

Romans 8:35

Adverbial Genitive

When the head or governing nominal suggests a verbal process, a genitive may
have an underlying *adverbial* role, in the sense of both the complement and adverbial accusative functions. It may, for example, be the patient/"do–ee," that is,
the recipient of a verbal process suggested in its governing nominal. It may, like
the adverbial adjunct accusative, convey a *circumstance* associated with a verbal
process that the governing nominal suggests.

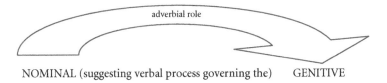

NOMINAL (suggesting verbal process governing the)   GENITIVE

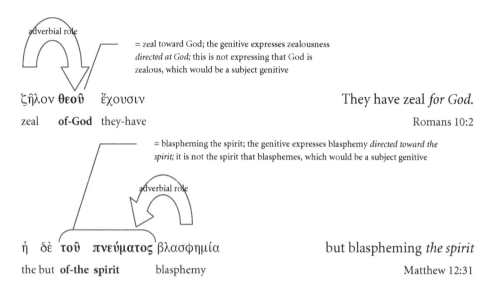

ζῆλον **θεοῦ** ἔχουσιν

zeal **of-God** they-have

= zeal toward God; the genitive expresses zealousness *directed at God;* this is not expressing that God is zealous, which would be a subject genitive

They have zeal *for God.*

Romans 10:2

= blaspheming the spirit; the genitive expresses blasphemy *directed toward the spirit;* it is not the spirit that blasphemes, which would be a subject genitive

ἡ δὲ **τοῦ πνεύματος** βλασφημία

the but **of-the spirit** blasphemy

but blaspheming *the spirit*

Matthew 12:31

Adjective Genitive

Here is the bulk of the genitive. The head or governing nominal and the genitive may modify each other, similarly to what adjectives do. Unlike the subject and adverbial genitive, the head or governing nominal of an adjective genitive usually does *not* suggest a verbal process.

The relationship between the head/governing nominal and the genitive may go in either direction. The genitive may modify the head/governing nominal, or the head/governing nominal may modify the genitive.

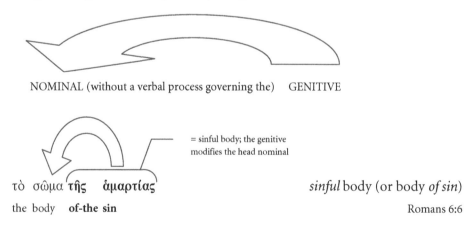

NOMINAL (without a verbal process governing the) GENITIVE

= sinful body; the genitive modifies the head nominal

τὸ σῶμα **τῆς ἁμαρτίας**

the body **of-the sin**

sinful body (or body *of sin*)

Romans 6:6

NOMINAL (without a verbal process governing the)   GENITIVE

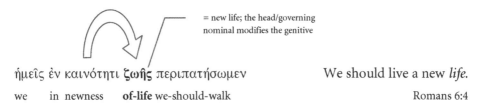

= new life; the head/governing
nominal modifies the genitive

ἡμεῖς ἐν καινότητι **ζωῆς** περιπατήσωμεν   We should live a new *life*.

we   in newness   **of-life** we-should-walk   Romans 6:4

Verb-Governed Genitive

The genitive is primarily an *adnominal* phenomenon; that is, a *nominal* governs
it. We see, however, that it can also be governed directly by a verb.

Some verbs, instead of governing complement accusatives, govern *complement
genitives*. Complement genitives are so-called because we consider them necessary
and a "complete-ment" of a verbal process. Verbs that convey notions of 'rule',
'sensation' (*hear, see, touch, taste*), 'accusation', and 'emotion' may take a complement genitive.

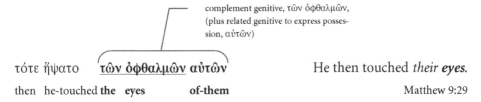

complement genitive, τῶν ὀφθαλμῶν,
(plus related genitive to express possession, αὐτῶν)

τότε ἥψατο   **τῶν ὀφθαλμῶν αὐτῶν**   He then touched *their **eyes***.

then he-touched **the eyes**   **of-them**   Matthew 9:29

We may also talk of an *adverbial adjunct genitive,* an adjunct to a verbal process
(as opposed to a complement). The genitive case may convey 'separation'—the
separative/ablative genitive. This same notion is routinely conveyed in Biblical
Greek by the adnominal construction of a preposition (ἐκ and ἀπό) governing a
nominal in the genitive case. Here, though, we are looking at the genitive governed by a verb.

53

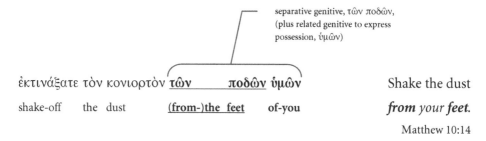

separative genitive, τῶν ποδῶν,
(plus related genitive to express
possession, ὑμῶν)

ἐκτινάξατε τὸν κονιορτὸν **τῶν** **ποδῶν** ὑμῶν

shake-off   the   dust   **(from-)the feet**   of-you

Shake the dust
from your feet.

Matthew 10:14

DATIVE CASE

Primarily related to the verbal process expressed in a clause, the dative case conveys *relation*. It is, like the accusative case but unlike the genitive, chiefly *adverbial* (linked "*to the verb*").

As we read first for the accusative, we need to keep in mind the distinction between adverbials that are *complements* and *adjuncts*. This allows us to talk of an adverbial complement, which we shall label a COMPLEMENT DATIVE, and a type of adverbial adjunct, which we shall call an ADVERBIAL ADJUNCT DATIVE. The latter is where we find the bulk of the dative's functions, and we shall talk about it first. Here is an illustration of how the dative relates to a clause (the accusative and the verb-governed genitive are included to help see the bigger picture).

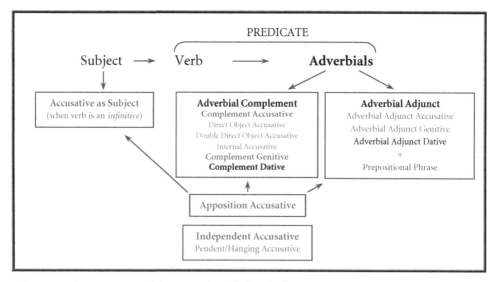

Figure 12: Select Functions of the Dative (with "Ghost" of Accusative and Verb-Governed Genitive)

54

Adverbial Adjunct

Adverbial Adjunct Dative

The relations that the dative conveys are principally these:

➤ **associative dative**—the expression of associations such as

- that to which a verbal process is given or done, often called the *dative of indirect object:* "give a gift *to her*"

  πάντα ἀποδώσω **σοι**   I will repay *you* everything.

  all-things I-will-repay **to-you**   Matthew 18:26

- advantage or disadvantage: "take a gift *for her*" or "hold a grudge *against him*"

  ἡ   δὲ Ἡρῳδιὰς ἐνεῖχεν   **αὐτῷ**   Herodias held a grudge

  (the) but Herodias   she-held-grudge **against-him**   *against him.*

  Mark 6:19

- reference: "the name (*with respect to him* or *referring to him*) was John"

  ὄνομα **αὐτῷ**   Ἰωάννης   *His* name was John.

  name   **referring-to-him** John   John 1:6

➤ **instrumental dative**—the means by which a verbal process happens

  οἱ δὲ ἄλλοι μαθηταὶ **τῷ**   **πλοιαρίῳ** ἦλθον   But the other disciples

  the but other   disciples **by-the little-boat**   they-came   came *by the little boat.*

  John 21:8

  κατακόπτων ἑαυτὸν **λίθοις**   gashing himself *with stones*

  gashing   himself **with-stones**   Mark 5:5

➤ **locative dative**—the location (time or place) or sphere where a verbal process takes place

  ἐπέθηκαν αὐτοῦ **τῇ**   **κεφαλῇ**   They put it *on his head.*

  they-placed of-him **on-the head**   John 19:2

καὶ τῇ τρίτῃ ἡμέρᾳ ἐγερθήσεται	*On the third day* he will be raised.
and **on-the third day** he-will-be-raised	Matthew 20:19

Adverbial Complement

Complement Dative

Complement datives are those that are considered necessary and a "complete-ment" of a verbal process. An underlying notion seems to connect the verbs that take complement datives: the verbs express close personal *relation*. The sense of relation, what many grammarians consider to be the *core* of the dative, conveyed in such verbs is in large part why the dative linked to these verbs is considered a complement rather than an adjunct. Verbs that commonly take complement datives express notions of 'worship', 'follow', 'trust', 'serve', and 'obey'.

ὑπακούουσιν **αὐτῷ**	They obey *him.*
they-obey **him**	Mark 1:27

We have now seen that Biblical Greek's adverbial complements can be in the accusative, genitive, or dative cases.

VOCATIVE CASE

Biblical Greek uses the vocative case in direct address, referring to an addressee. We saw that the nominative also did this in the appellative (direct address) nominative.

θεέ μου θεέ μου	My *God*, my *God*
God of-me **God** of-me	Matthew 27:46

VERB

A **VERB** is a word that conveys a process, whether full of action or static (for example, *seem* or *be*). In the chapter **SEMANTICS: PROCESSES, ROLES, AND CIRCUMSTANCES**, we talk about three primary spheres of verbal processes: the *material* = doing, the *mental* = sensing, and the *relational*. See p. 203.

Here are some basic concepts closely associated with verbs.

FINITE AND NONFINITE

A verb is considered **FINITE** if it *can occur on its own in an independent or main clause* and conveys *person, aspect/tense,* and *mood*. In Biblical Greek the finite verbal forms are those that are *not* infinitives or participles.

A verb is considered **NONFINITE** if it can*not* occur on its own in an independent or main clause and does *not* convey person, aspect/tense, and mood. In Biblical Greek the infinitives and participles are nonfinite verbal forms.

TRANSITIVE AND INTRANSITIVE

A **TRANSITIVE** verb governs a direct object (direct object accusative). Such a verb tends to be fientive (see this concept below).

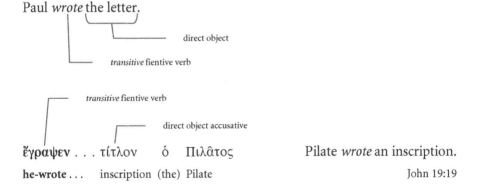

Paul *wrote* the letter.
direct object
transitive fientive verb

transitive fientive verb
direct object accusative

ἔγραψεν . . . τίτλον   ὁ   Πιλᾶτος

he-wrote . . .   inscription (the) Pilate

Pilate *wrote* an inscription.

John 19:19

An **INTRANSITIVE** verb does not govern a direct object.

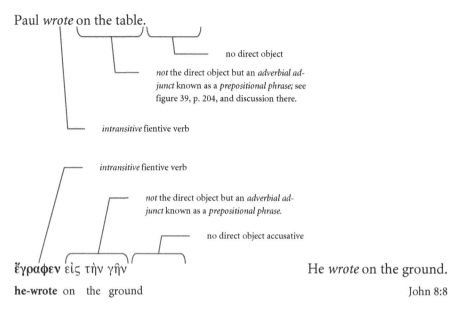

Paul *wrote* on the table.

no direct object

not the direct object but an *adverbial adjunct* known as a *prepositional phrase;* see figure 39, p. 204, and discussion there.

intransitive fientive verb

intransitive fientive verb

not the direct object but an *adverbial adjunct* known as a *prepositional phrase.*

no direct object accusative

ἔγραφεν εἰς τὴν γῆν
he-wrote on the ground

He *wrote* on the ground.

John 8:8

FIENTIVE AND STATIVE

A **FIENTIVE** verb conveys activity or a dynamic situation. The verb may be *transitive.*

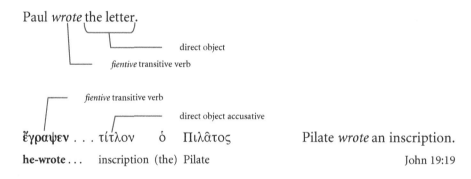

Paul *wrote* the letter.

direct object

fientive transitive verb

fientive transitive verb

direct object accusative

ἔγραψεν . . . τίτλον ὁ Πιλᾶτος
he-wrote . . . inscription (the) Pilate

Pilate *wrote* an inscription.

John 19:19

58

Or it may be intransitive.

Paul *wrote* on the table.

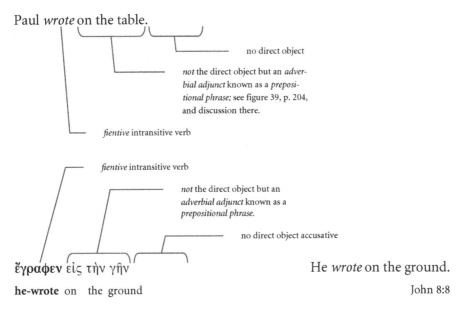

no direct object

not the direct object but an *adverbial adjunct* known as a *prepositional phrase; see figure 39, p. 204,* and discussion there.

fientive intransitive verb

fientive intransitive verb

not the direct object but an *adverbial adjunct* known as a prepositional phrase.

no direct object accusative

ἔγραφεν εἰς τὴν γῆν

he-wrote on the ground

He *wrote* on the ground.

John 8:8

Fientive contrasts with *stative*.

A **STATIVE** verb denotes a state, circumstance, or quality. Most statives are intransitive.

I *am*.

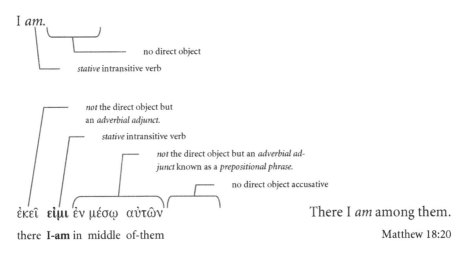

no direct object

stative intransitive verb

not the direct object but an *adverbial adjunct*.

stative intransitive verb

not the direct object but an *adverbial adjunct* known as a *prepositional phrase.*

no direct object accusative

ἐκεῖ εἰμι ἐν μέσῳ αὐτῶν

there I-am in middle of-them

There I *am* among them.

Matthew 18:20

59

TENSE AND ASPECT

Understanding TENSE and ASPECT is fundamental to understanding the Greek verbal system. English speakers are comfortable talking about their language from a perspective of tense: present tense, past tense, etc. ASPECT is a concept not very familiar to English speakers. Ironically, though, English has numerous constructions that convey it. Aspect, in fact, to some extent, is fused with the English verbal system.

Grammarians of Biblical Greek debate, at times quite vigorously, the respective roles that tense and aspect play within the language. The view here is that *aspect* plays the most *fundamental* role in the Biblical Greek verbal system. We therefore need to understand tense and especially aspect.

ENGLISH

TENSE

TENSE denotes *when* the process of a verb takes place. We can talk about ABSOLUTE and RELATIVE tense.

Absolute Tense

Absolute tense relates the TIME of a situation from the speaker's PRESENT. English has three *major* absolute tenses: PAST, PRESENT, and FUTURE. Each of these has subcategories, which we shall explore. The illustration below can help us to conceptualize the absolute tenses. Each circle represents a situation, and the vertical line represents the moment of speaking or writing.

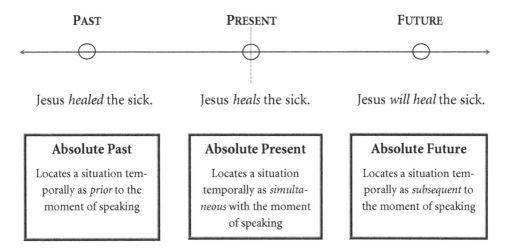

Figure 13: English Absolute Tense

To each of these, we can add the notion of **PROGRESSION**: a situation, relative to the moment of speaking, is viewed as being *in progress*. A type of aspect, to which we shall soon turn, is conveyed in English through progression.

➤ Absolute Past Progressive: Jesus *was healing* the sick.

➤ Absolute Present Progressive: Jesus *is healing* the sick.

➤ Absolute Future Progressive: Jesus *will be healing* the sick.

Relative Tense

Relative tense relates the TIME of a situation to the TIME OF ANOTHER SITUATION. Conceptualize the situation of *walking down the road.*

> ➤ Relative Past Tense: When walking down the road, Jesus *healed* the sick.

> ➤ Relative Present Tense: When walking down the road, Jesus *heals* the sick.

> ➤ Relative Future Tense: When walking down the road, Jesus *will heal* the sick.

ASPECT

ASPECT is a concept not very familiar to English speakers, but, as I said above, the language has numerous constructions that convey it (progression, for example). Aspect is the view on the ***internal*** *structure of a situation* (most any circumstance you can envision can be thought of as a situation). The categories of aspect I discuss below are the PERFECTIVE, IMPERFECTIVE, and RESULTATIVE/STATIVE (better known as the "perfect" in English grammars). (We could talk of other categories.) Whereas the first two, perfective and imperfective, are, without doubt, categories of aspect, many debate whether the resultative/stative should be a category of aspect. It is somewhat different, as we shall see, from the first two. In brief, the resultative/stative usually focuses on a continuing relevance of a past situation. I follow those who believe the resultative/stative best belongs with aspect.

English does not have a special form of the verb to distinguish tense from aspect. Some languages—Slavic ones, for example—do have special forms. Most linguists who study Biblical Greek believe that aspect plays a fundamental role in the Greek verbal system. In English we shall try to understand aspect by exploring the meanings our many different so-called "tenses" are trying to convey.

Perfective Aspect (Perfectivity)

The perfective aspect, or perfectivity, views *a situation from the **outside**, as whole and complete.* Think of the situation of Junia having read a scroll yesterday and conceptualize it as a sphere.

Situation: The reading of the scroll by Junia yesterday

Express the situation in English as the sentence "Junia read the scroll yesterday." The sentence, when viewed from the standpoint of PERFECTIVE ASPECT, expresses the *totality* of the situation, with*out* dividing up its internal temporal structure. The *whole* situation is presented as an undivided whole. The beginning, middle, and end are rolled up into one. To help understand this, think of the many things Junia could have done yesterday in between reading the scroll: walking to and from her home, eating lunch, etc. The perfective aspect is not concerned with any of that—it makes no attempt to divide the situation into various phases.

Now think of the situation of Junia reading the scroll tomorrow. Again, think of that situation as a sphere.

Situation: The reading of the scroll by Junia tomorrow

The English expression "Junia will read the scroll tomorrow," when viewed from the standpoint of PERFECTIVE ASPECT, still expresses the *totality* of the situation, with*out* dividing up its internal temporal structure, even though the situation has not yet occurred. The *whole* situation is still presented as an undivided whole.

English speakers, when we read such sentences, most likely see them from a standpoint of TENSE. Indeed, they *can* be viewed from the perspective of tense: one situation is oriented temporally prior to the present; the other, temporally anterior. Aspect, however, is *another* way to view a situation. The perfective aspect sees a situation as whole without considering how it relates in time to the present. It looks at a situation, further, *without* specifying how component parts of the situation (for example, reading a scroll at different times through the day, going to lunch, etc.) relate within the whole situation.

Here are more examples of what perfectivity entails:

➤ Single or momentary situations

I *repaired* the wall.

He *will write* the message and *send* it to Corinth.

➤ Situations that have a goal of completion

Did you *finish repairing* the wall?

Will she *memorize* the paradigm?

What *did* you *do* yesterday? (what was *accomplished?*)
— I *sacrificed* a ram. (*whole* situation)
— And I *worked* in the garden. (*whole* situation)

What *will* you *do* tomorrow? (what will be *accomplished?*)
— I *shall sacrifice* a ram. (*whole* situation)
— And I *shall work* in the garden. (*whole* situation)

Again, English speakers will automatically see these sentences expressing past and future tense. From the view of perfective aspect, however, they are situations viewed as a whole.

Imperfective Aspect (Imperfectivity)

The imperfective aspect, or imperfectivity, views *a situation's **insides**. It considers the internal temporal structure of a situation.* Think again of our situation of Junia reading the scroll.

Situation: The reading of the scroll by Junia

Consider the following sentences linked to our situation:

1. Junia read the scroll yesterday.

2. While she was reading it, one of the Roman congregants arrived.

In English, again, we can view the sentences from a perspective of either tense or aspect. From an ASPECTUAL perspective, sentence 1 is perfective: the situation is viewed from the outside and is whole, complete. Sentence 2, however, opens up the situation and says that at some time during the situation of Junia reading her scroll, one of the Roman congregants arrived. From a perspective of TENSE, sentence 1 is absolute past tense. The first (and subordinate) clause in sentence 2 is absolute past progressive, while the second (and main clause) is relative past.

Here are more examples of what imperfectivity entails:

➢ Repeated or habitual situations

I *studied* Biblical Greek every day.

He *will* never *repair* the wall.

She *would bake* the flat bread every morning.

➢ Situations in progress (thus not complete) (notice the idea of *progression,* which English can commonly convey)

They *were working* when he entered.

They *will be working* when he enters.

➢ Completed situations without a view to result

What *did* you *do* yesterday? (what *activity* took place?)
— I *sacrificed* a ram. (view on *activity*)
— And I *worked* in the garden. (view on *activity*)

Compare this last example with the next-to-last example in the perfective-aspect section. The sentences are identical. They can be viewed quite differently, however, from an aspectual perspective.

Perfect "Aspect" = Resultative/Stative

The RESULTATIVE/STATIVE presents a view of a STATE that is usually the result of a PRECEDING SITUATION. English speakers know it better as the "perfect." Here is a way to conceptualize it.

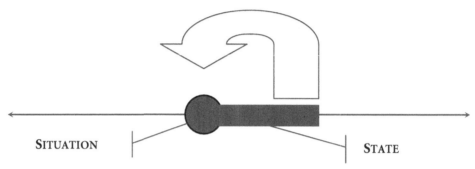

Figure 14: The Resultative/Stative

Stated a bit more precisely, the resultative/stative expresses (1) a state resulting from a prior situation and (2) in English, the time of the prior situation.

Not everyone agrees whether the resultative/stative in English is best regarded as a tense, aspect, or something else. Here we classify it as an aspect, in part because it involves the perfective aspect. The *situation* in the resultative/stative is represented through the perfective aspect. In addition, however, to incorporating perfectivity to represent a situation, the resultative/stative expresses a *state* resulting from that situation.

In English, we commonly combine the resultative/stative with *time*. This sets the stage for different types of resultative/statives related to time. (We shall use the label *perfect*, used commonly in English grammars.)

➢ Past Perfect/Pluperfect: Jesus *had eaten.*

The past perfect expresses a PAST abiding STATE relating to a PRIOR SITUATION. The situation of *eating* is complete (perfective) and has been accomplished in the past, and the state of having eaten continued for a time prior to the moment of speaking.

➤ Present Perfect: Jesus *has eaten.*

The present perfect expresses a **PRESENT** abiding **STATE** from a **PRIOR SITUA-TION.** The situation of *eating* is complete (perfective) and has been accomplished in the past, while the state of having eaten continues to the moment of speaking.

➤ Future Perfect: Jesus *will have eaten.*

The future perfect expresses a **FUTURE** abiding **STATE** relating to a **PRIOR SITUATION.** The situation of *eating* will be complete (perfective) and will be accomplished in the future, and the state of having eaten will continue for a time subsequent to the moment of speaking.

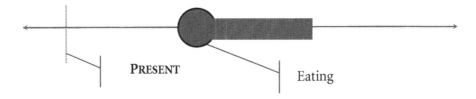

To each of these we can add the notion of **PROGRESSION.**

67

> Past Perfect/Pluperfect Progressive: Jesus *had been eating.*

> Present Perfect Progressive: Jesus *has been eating.*

> Future Perfect Progressive: Jesus *will have been eating.*

Aktionsart

You may encounter in your grammar or secondary readings the German word *Aktionsart* (literally, "action-type"). Some grammars simply use the English phrase, "kind of action."

We do not find agreement among linguists on the relationship of *Aktionsart* to aspect. Linguists do agree that verbal processes can convey concepts such as *habit/custom* ("she *would [customarily] fast* once a week"), *iterativity* (= repeated process, "she *jumped several times*"), *voice* (active, middle, or passive [see Voice, p. 98]), *stativity* or *fientivity* (see under Verb at p. 58), etc.

Some bundle all of the above as categories of Aspect. Others bundle all of the above as categories of **Aktionsart**. Yet others tie together *habit/custom* and *iterativity* and add *punctuality/momentariness* (describing a brief verbal process in its entirety) and *inception* (describing the *beginning* of a verbal process) as categories of Aspect but group *voice, stativity/fientivity,* and *transitivity* as categories of *Aktionsart.*

As you read grammars and other linguistic helps, you will need to decipher how an author is using "aspect" and *"Aktionsart."* You may also perhaps bemoan why we who write about languages cannot agree on what seem to be basics and that we do not write more clearly, try as we might.

Biblical Greek

Tense

Does the Biblical Greek verbal system primarily convey tense or aspect? The issue is not unimportant. Let us look, for example, at a theologically significant verse.

εἰ	δὲ	ἐν	δακτύλῳ	θεοῦ	[ἐγὼ]	**ἐκβάλλω**	τὰ	δαιμόνια,
if	but	by	finger	of-God	I	**I-drive-out**	the	demons

ἄρα ἔφθασεν ἐφ᾽ ὑμᾶς ἡ βασιλεία τοῦ θεοῦ
then **she-came** on you the kingdom of(-the) God

> But if it is by the finger of God that I drive out demons, then the Kingdom of God has come on you (*or* has caught you unaware). Luke 11:20

What are we to make of an aorist indicative (ἔφθασεν) referring to the coming of God's kingdom occurring after a present indicative (ἐκβάλλω)? Initially, many students learn that the aorist commonly conveys the past and that the present conveys the present—a tense-oriented understanding. But what might this be saying if Biblical Greek's verbal system is primarily aspectual? The ramifications are significant.

Linguists of Biblical Greek debate whether the verbal system truly conveys tense. We must first, though, be very careful to clarify how the term *tense* is commonly used in the discipline.

Tense, almost universally in Biblical Greek, is a label, that is, a word that refers to each of the following verbal forms: present, aorist, imperfect, future, perfect, and pluperfect—the Biblical Greek so-called "tenses." Depending on the resource you are reading, you need to discover whether the use of the word tense *also* understands the forms truly to be tenses. At the very least, this use has become a standard way to talk about Biblical Greek *verbal forms*.

The term tense also might be used by grammars to refer to the concept of *when* a verbal process takes place, *separate from* or *part of* the labeling of the so-called tenses.

You, as a reader, must be very careful to understand how a particular author uses a term each time he or she mentions it. This book uses *tense* primarily to refer to the concept of situating a verbal process in time. Throughout the book, when I refer to the so-called Biblical Greek tenses, I use the label *"tense"-form:* for example, present "tense"-form, aorist "tense"-form, etc.[20]

---

[20] The idea for this labeling comes from Stanley Porter in, for example, *Idioms of the Greek New Testament* (2d ed.; Biblical Languages: Greek 2; Sheffield: Sheffield Academic Press, 1994).

I said above that linguists of Biblical Greek debate the extent the verbal system conveys tense and/or aspect. Let us try to understand some of the principal points.

The debate focuses on the indicative mood (see the sections on **REAL MOOD** = **INDICATIVE MOOD** for English and Biblical Greek, pp. 82 and 89 respectively). We find general agreement that time/tense is not an issue in the non-indicative moods (subjunctive, optative, imperative).

Most grammarians agree that **DISCOURSE** (a "chunk" of text; see p. 6) that contains indicative-mood finite verbs can commonly convey *time,* that is, convey *when* a verbal process takes place. The disagreement centers around whether the indicative verb forms *themselves* convey tense or whether a verbal process is tethered to time *secondarily* by other elements in the discourse, such as adverbs of time.

Finding a way forward through the debate is not easy. Some of the finest minds in the discipline, after all, do not agree with each other. Here are some of the complicating factors:

- Language changes through time. What is true for a language in a given moment in time is not necessarily true of its past or of what will be its future. (Have you read *Beowulf* in Old English recently, or Chaucer's Middle English *Canterbury Tales?*)

- Koine Greek, within which Biblical Greek is but a specific textual corpus, was embraced by myriads of non-Greek-speaking peoples. For many, it was a learned language, augmenting a mother tongue. It is not unlikely that many writers, knowingly or unknowingly, altered Greek, shaping it to express similarities to their mother tongues—aspect-oriented mother tongues shaping Greek toward aspect, or tense-oriented mother tongues shaping Greek toward tense (which would it be?).

- Even individual writers within the Biblical Greek corpus may understand and use the Greek verbal system differently.

- Verbal processes themselves vary greatly. A major semantic distinction is between (1) *fientive/dynamic verbs,* conveying activity, and (2) *stative verbs,* describing state-of-being. Stative verbs, by definition, convey durative and positional processes (εἰμί *be*). Not being aware of this semantic distinction can confuse our notions of verbal processes. Imperfective aspect sees verbal processes, in part, as progressions, durations—already what stative verbs convey without being cast into an imperfective aspect. What, furthermore, are the roles of perfective aspect for stative verbs?

Biblical Greek, as a discipline, needs to develop a better understanding of how such complexities inform our view of the verbal system.

We shall, nevertheless, suggest that tense is *not* a concept fundamentally linked to the Biblical Greek verb forms *themselves.* The verbal system itself, in all moods, is fundamentally an *aspectual* system. (This is not to say, however, that, in instances, a particular writer is using a verbal form to convey tense. We cannot be certain that all users of Greek, acquired from parents or learned later in life, use the language consistently with other users.)

That Biblical Greek verb forms *themselves* more fundamentally convey aspect does not mean, however, that Biblical Greek cannot tell time! In all moods, if the time of a situation is to be conveyed, the verbal form *in conjunction with other elements in the discourse* root the situation in time. Temporal information is conveyed primarily through the discourse around a verb in question.

Here are examples of the present "tense"-form (which we shall see below normally conveys IMPERFECTIVE ASPECT), all in the indicative mood (because this mood is where the disagreement centers on how aspect and tense operate), referring to different temporal situations. The time being conveyed is understood from the total package of the verb *along with* the discourse surrounding the verb. (I have not, because of space, included the full textual environment with these examples.)

71

➢ Present "tense"-form conveying present time

Καίσαρα	ἐπικαλοῦμαι	To Caesar *I appeal.*
Caesar	**I-appeal**	Acts 25:11

➢ Present "tense"-form conveying past time

καὶ **ἔρχεται** πρὸς τοὺς μαθητὰς	He *came* to the disciples and *found*
and **he-comes** to the disciples	them sleeping. He *said* to Peter . . .
καὶ **εὑρίσκει** αὐτοὺς καθεύδοντας	Matthew 26:40
and **he-finds** them sleeping	
καὶ **λέγει** τῷ Πέτρῳ	
and **he-says** to(-the) Peter	

➢ Present "tense"-form conveying future time

Ἠλίας μὲν **ἔρχεται** καὶ ἀποκαταστήσει πάντα	Elijah *is coming* and
Elijah indeed **he-comes** and he-restores all	will restore all things.
	Matthew 17:11

➢ Present "tense"-form conveying any time (*omnitemporal* or *gnomic:* a verbal process that does not focus primarily on *when* it occurs but that it *does* occur, often routinely)

τὸ πνεῦμα ὅπου θέλει **πνεῖ**	The wind *blows* where it wishes.
the wind where it-wishes **it-blows**	John 3:8

These examples show how one "tense"-form conveys a full variety of temporal situations. Such a phenomenon helps us to see that a "tense"-form is probably best seen as conveying ASPECT (here IMPERFECTIVITY), *not* tense that conveys temporality. Indeed, as a further example, we see that the aorist "tense"-form can refer to situations in past, present, and future time.[21] The *aspectual* perspective of the Biblical Greek verbal system can be rooted in *time* by clues from the surrounding discourse.

---

[21] For a multitude of examples of how each "tense"-form can refer to a range of *time*, see Daniel B. Wallace, *The Basics of New Testament Syntax: An Intermediate Greek Grammar* (Grand Rapids, Mich.: Zondervan, 2000), 213–53; Wallace, *Greek Grammar*, 494–586; Porter, *Idioms*, 29–45.

It is quite easy, though, to understand why we can be tempted to see the Biblical Greek verbal system as fundamentally tense-oriented. Take the aorist "tense"-form, for example. Commonly we see the aorist in textual environments that convey situations in past time. Past *tense*, right? Well, likely no, though we cannot dismiss the possibility that some individual writers might have had tense in mind. Users of Biblical Greek, rather, seem to have considered the aorist, which conveys perfectivity, a *whole* or *complete* situation, as logically compatible for routinely conveying a *complete* situation in the past. This, however, is not tense at work. Remember that the big picture of the aorist "tense"-form shows that it can refer to situations rooted in time to the past *and* present *and* future. The aorist "tense"-form is perfective *aspect* used for different temporal situations.

ASPECT

I said previously that the Biblical Greek verbal system, in all moods, is fundamentally an *aspectual* system. We turn our attention now to see how the "tense"-forms match up with the three major aspects in Biblical Greek: PERFECTIVE, IMPERFECTIVE, and RESULTATIVE/STATIVE. This is an overview. We shall have a separate discussion about the future "tense"-form in a separate section.

ASPECT:	PERFECTIVE	IMPERFECTIVE	RESULTATIVE/STATIVE
"Tense"-Form:	Aorist	Present Imperfect	Perfect Pluperfect

Figure 15: Aspect and Biblical Greek "Tense"-Forms

Perfective Aspect (Perfectivity)

The aorist "tense"-form conveys PERFECTIVE ASPECT.

μετὰ δὲ τρεῖς μῆνας **ἀνήχθημεν** ἐν πλοίῳ   Then after three months
after then three months **we-set-sail** in ship   *we set sail* in a ship . . .

Acts 28:11

ταύτην τὴν ἐντολὴν **ἔλαβον**   This charge *I have received . . .*

this   the command **I-have-received**   John 10:18

εἰς   τοῦτο γὰρ Χριστὸς **ἀπέθανεν** καὶ **ἔζησεν**   It was for this purpose

concerning this   for Christ   **he-died**   and **he-became-alive**   Christ *died* and

became alive (again).

Romans 14:9

ἐξηράνθη   ὁ   χόρτος καὶ τὸ ἄνθος **ἐξέπεσεν**   The grass *withers* and

he-withers   the grass   and the flower **it-falls-off**   the blossom *falls.*

1 Peter 1:24

ἰδοὺ **ἦλθεν**   κύριος ἐν   ἁγίαις μυριάσιν αὐτοῦ The Lord *is going to come*

look **he-is-coming** Lord   with saints   myriad   of-him with his countless saints.

Jude 14

Here you can notice the variety of tenses and other nuances we use in English to convey the perfective aspect of the aorist "tense"-form.

Commonly we see the aorist in textual environments that convey situations in past time. Remember that users of Biblical Greek seem to have considered the aorist, which conveys perfectivity—a *whole* or *complete* situation—as compatible for routinely conveying a *complete* situation in the past. This, however, is not tense. The aorist shows that it can refer to situations rooted in time to the past *and* present *and* future. The aorist is perfective aspect used for different temporal situations.

Imperfective Aspect (Imperfectivity)

The present and the imperfect "tense"-forms convey IMPERFECTIVE ASPECT.

Present "Tense"-Form

ἀλήθειαν **λέγω** ἐν Χριστῷ   I *am telling* you the truth in Christ.

truth   **I-say** in Christ   Romans 9:1

καὶ	εἰσπορεύονται	εἰς	Καφαρναούμ	They *entered* Capernaum.
and	**they-enter**	into	Capernaum	Mark 1:21

This last example is one of a myriad of instances where the present "tense"-form conveys a verbal process that happened in the past. Grammars refer to this commonly as the *historical present*. They say that using the present "tense"-form in such a fashion seems, in part, to be a way to enrich the verbal process. It is a way of trying to express the phenomenon that language can evoke or suppress emotion; language can be extremely dynamic, or not be. We can pause again to reflect that the verb is not conveying tense/time but imperfective *aspect*. Here now are other functions of the present "tense"-form.

νηστεύω	δὶς	τοῦ	σαββάτου	I *customarily fast* twice a week.
I-fast	twice	the	Sabbath	Luke 18:12

Ἠλίας	μὲν	**ἔρχεται**	καὶ	ἀποκαταστήσει	πάντα	Elijah *is coming* and will
Elijah	indeed	**he-comes**	and	he-will-restore	all	restore all things.
						Matthew 17:11

Notice the variety of tenses—present, past, future—we use in English to convey the imperfective *aspect* of the present "tense"-form.

Imperfect "Tense"-Form

The imperfect "tense"-form conveys imperfective aspect very often in textual environments that envision the past. The aorist, remember, is also commonly found in contexts envisioning the past. The difference is *aspect*. The aorist is encapsulating verbal processes from a *perfective* viewpoint, while the imperfect is offering an *imperfective* viewpoint.

ὁ	Φαρισαῖος	σταθεὶς	πρὸς	ἑαυτὸν	ταῦτα	**προσηύχετο**	The Pharisee stood
the	Pharisee	standing	to	himself	these-things	**he-was-praying**	and *was praying* this to himself.
							Luke 18:11

75

πεσὼν ἐπὶ τῆς γῆς	**ἐκυλίετο**	ἀφρίζων	He fell on the ground
fall(en) on the ground	**he-began-rolling**	foaming	and *began rolling around*,
			foaming at the mouth.
			Mark 9:20

ἔλεγον,	Χαῖρε ὁ βασιλεὺς τῶν ᾿Ιουδαίων		They *kept on saying*,
they-kept-saying	hail the king of-the Jews		"Hail, King of the Jews!"
			John 19:3

σάββατον **ἐπέφωσκεν**	The Sabbath *was about to begin*.
Sabbath **it-was-dawning**	Luke 23:54

Resultative/Stative "Aspect"

The perfect and the pluperfect "tense"-forms convey RESULTATIVE/STATIVE "AS-
PECT." It expresses, remember, a state *usually* (but not always) resulting from a
prior situation. The focus, in Biblical Greek, appears to be primarily on the resultant *state*. This resultant state is what distinguishes it from other "tense"-forms.

Perfect "Tense"-Form

The perfect "tense"-form is used far less frequently than the aorist, present, and
imperfect "tense"-forms.

"in whom you are in
a *state* of hoping."

εἰς ὃν	ὑμεῖς **ἠλπίκατε**		in whom you *hope*
in whom	you **you-hope**		John 5:45

ἡ ἀγάπη τοῦ	θεοῦ **ἐκκέχυται**		The love of God
the love of(-the) God	**she-has-been-poured-out**		*has been poured out*.
			Romans 5:5

"The love of God is in a *state* of
having been poured out."

Pluperfect "Tense"-Form

Like the imperfect "tense"-form, the pluperfect "tense"-form conveys its aspect very often in textual environments that envision the past.

ἤδη γὰρ **συνετέθειντο** οἱ Ἰουδαῖοι   For the Jews *had already agreed.*

already for **they-had-agreed** the Jews   John 9:22

"The Jews had already come into
a *state* of agreeing."

THE FUTURE "TENSE"-FORM: A SPECIAL CHALLENGE

If the Biblical Greek "tense"-forms up to this point have tested your understanding, the future "tense"-form offers a further challenge.

We find a wide range of thoughts about this form. Some see it as a *tense* referring to a situation subsequent to the moment of speaking. Others view the form as a blend of *perfective aspect* and *future tense*. Some see the verbal form as another *mood*, alongside the indicative, subjunctive, etc.—future "tense"-forms and subjunctive forms (there is no future subjunctive) often appear in similar textual environments. One view holds that the form holds a unique place in the Biblical Greek verbal system, being vague regarding aspect but clear for expressing *expectation* for a situation to occur.

With reservation, my own preference lies with the last view. I particularly echo the "unique" characteristic mentioned in the view. The future "tense"-form, in general, seems sometimes to refer to what is not yet, sometimes to convey a command (and thus is like a mood), and sometimes to express expectation and intention for something to occur.

IMPERATIVE: 2D & 3D PERSON

The **IMPERATIVE**, a **MOOD**, imposes the will of a speaker onto an entity. You need to read the entire chapter on **MOOD** (p. 81) to understand how the imperative fits into the bigger picture of mood.

ENGLISH

The **IMPERATIVE**, in some circles, is also known as the **VOLITIONAL MOOD**. It is considered *irreal* because the speaker's desire depends on whether the addressee will accede to the speaker's will. The speaker's will is thus not actual or *real* unless the addressee performs what the speaker desires. In anticipation of looking at Biblical Greek, we can talk about two different types of volitional moods, or *volitives:* 2d and 3d person volition.

2d Person Volition

SECOND PERSON VOLITION is better known among English speakers as the **IMPERATIVE**. The speaker wishes to impose his or her will on the grammatical 2d person. The order may be to one person or several people. The imperative commonly uses the dictionary form of the verb but no 2d person subject pronoun (see **PRONOUN**, p. 121), though it may occur.

> *Bow* before the Procurator!
>
> *Sit* here!
>
> You, *stop* that!

English acrolect (the prestige dialect) also expresses the imperative by *you shall + verb*. By contrast, *you will + verb* expresses the future tense (see **TENSE**, p. 60) of the indicative mood. Few English speakers keep this distinction clear.[22]

---

[22] As I mentioned in the introduction, within the halls of the academy, the commonest surroundings I envision for this textbook, it is pedagogically useful to use English's acrolect, its *prestige* forms, while pointing out pertinent *colloquial* forms. The academy, on occasion, still expects the acrolect of its students.

*You **shall** keep* the Sabbath! (= 2d person volition = imperative)

> The speaker is imposing his or her will on the addressee. The addressee is expected to obey the order.

*You **will** keep* the Sabbath. (= indicative mood)

> The speaker is simply stating actuality.

3d Person Volition

In **3D PERSON VOLITION** the speaker wishes to impose his or her will on the grammatical 3d person, singular or plural.

May YHWH bless you!

Let him pass!

Long live Caesar! (= *May Caesar live!*)

Let them enter Jerusalem!

BIBLICAL GREEK

Biblical Greek expresses the imperative mood in the 2d and 3d persons. Negative imperatives or **PROHIBITIONS** are routinely formed by μή (or related form) placed before the imperative, most commonly the *present "tense"-form* imperative.

Our view is that Biblical Greek's verbal system is fundamentally aspectual (see the chapter **TENSE AND ASPECT**, p. 60). The aorist "tense"-form imperative, as *perfective* aspect, conveys the verbal process as an undivided *whole* or *totality,* with*out* dividing up the internal temporal structure needed to accomplish it. The present "tense"-form imperative, as *imperfective* aspect, conveys the verbal process from the *inside,* considering the *process,* that is, the internal temporal structure needed to achieve it.

IMPERATIVE 2D PERSON

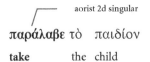

aorist 2d singular

παράλαβε τὸ παιδίον

take the child

Take the child.

Matthew 2:13

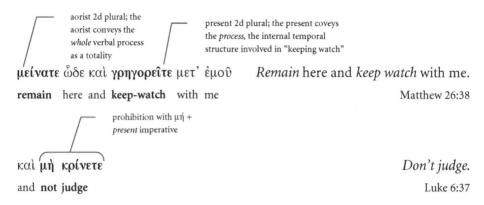

aorist 2d plural; the
aorist conveys the
whole verbal process
as a totality

present 2d plural; the present coveys
the *process*, the internal temporal
structure involved in "keeping watch"

μείνατε ὧδε καὶ γρηγορεῖτε μετ᾽ ἐμοῦ   *Remain* here and *keep watch* with me.

remain here and **keep-watch** with me   Matthew 26:38

prohibition with μή +
present imperative

καὶ **μὴ κρίνετε**   *Don't judge.*

and **not judge**   Luke 6:37

The last example leads to an important observation. When Biblical Greek wishes to prohibit, using μή plus the aorist "tense"-form, it does *not* use an aorist *imperative*. The language, rather, uses μὴ plus an aorist *subjunctive* (see below, **PROHIBITIVE SUBJUNCTIVE**, p. 93).

IMPERATIVE 3D PERSON

With Biblical Greek's 3d person imperative, we encounter a bit of disparity in how English routinely translates it. English conveys the 3d person imperative commonly in the form of the *permissive* or the *jussive:* "*Let* him/her *go, stand, stay,* etc." (See the chapter **TRANSLATION**, p. 20, which discusses **FORM** and **MEANING**.) This English phenomenon sounds less direct to an English speaker. Biblical Greek's 3d person imperative is, however, every bit as direct as its 2d person imperative.

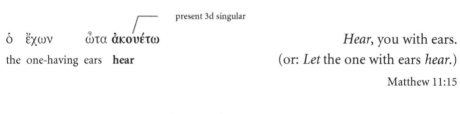

present 3d singular

ὁ ἔχων   ὦτα **ἀκουέτω**   *Hear,* you with ears.

the one-having ears **hear**   (or: *Let* the one with ears *hear.*)

                                           Matthew 11:15

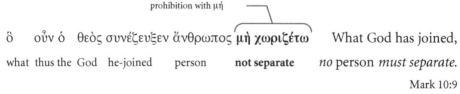

prohibition with μή

ὃ   οὖν ὁ   θεὸς συνέζευξεν ἄνθρωπος **μὴ χωριζέτω**   What God has joined,

what thus the God he-joined   person   **not separate**   *no* person *must separate.*

                                           Mark 10:9

MOOD

MOOD or MODALITY is the attitude or disposition a speaker has toward what she or he is expressing. Mood reflects the speaker's *mood*, as it were. A speaker can *declare* that an event happened (truthfully or untruthfully). She can *command, demand, wish* that something, which hasn't occurred, ought to occur. She can *prohibit* an action, which hasn't occurred, from happening.

With English and Biblical Greek in mind, we can categorize moods into two major divisions. Some prefer to use the labels

(1) REAL and (2) IRREAL;

others prefer the labels

(1) ACTUAL and (2) POTENTIAL. I shall use the first set.

In the first paragraph above, the concept of 'declare' is a real or actual mood. The rest of the concepts, 'command', 'demand', 'wish', 'prohibit' are different expressions within the irreal or potential mood.

Mood, *expressed through particular **verb** forms,* reflects a speaker's disposition toward whether a verbal process is real (or actual) or irreal (or potential).

In Biblical Greek we can talk of four distinct verbal forms that convey four distinct moods. We do not have the same picture in English. English can convey something similar to what Biblical Greek means by its four moods, but it does so in different fashion. The English and Biblical Greek sections below, therefore, will have a slightly different organization.

ENGLISH

We refer to the real mood generally as the INDICATIVE MOOD.

Under the irreal moods we focus our attention on many different possible situations. We shall categorize the irreal moods as the VOLITIONAL and the NONVOLITIONAL. In the former, the speaker imposes his or her will on an addressee. In the latter, the speaker expresses an attitude about a situation without imposing his or her will. The SUBJUNCTIVE MOOD fits here. English also uses a variety of *modal auxiliaries* (*may, should, ought, can, might, must,* etc.), which we shall call "MO-DALS," to convey attitudes such as PERMISSION (*may*), OBLIGATION (*should, ought*), CAPABILITY (*can*), POSSIBILITY (*might*), NECESSITY (*must*), DELIBERATION (*should?*), etc. Rather than have special verb forms that express attitudes such as permission, etc., English adds these "modals" into the clause along with a verb.

We thus have the following:

    (1) Real Mood = Indicative Mood

    (2) Irreal Mood

        (a) Volitional Mood

        (b) Nonvolitional Mood

            (i) Subjunctive Mood

            (ii) "Modals"

                a) Permission

                b) Obligation

                c) Capability

                d) Possibility

                e) Necessity

                f) Deliberation, etc.

REAL MOOD = INDICATIVE MOOD

Also known as the DECLARATIVE mood because it *declares,* the real or indicative mood customarily does the following:

➢ *asserts* (what is intended to be understood as) a fact:

    Jesus *lived* in Nazareth.

    Paul *is* in Antioch.

    Paul *will return* to Jerusalem.

• and, closely related, *probes* for information, often expecting an assertion in return:

    Are you the king?

> *asserts* a condition based on intended fact:

If Peter *is* in Rome, you will meet him.

> If the condition is real that Peter is in Rome, you, therefore, can meet him. (The subordinate clause, "If Peter *is* in Rome," asserts the condition, the focus of this function of the indicative; the other clause [the main clause], "you *will meet* him," asserts what is intended to be fact, the first function of the indicative mentioned above.)

The list is hardly exhaustive. The indicative conveys a verbal process that meshes with the speaker's perception of reality and his or her intent to have the hearer understand reality accordingly. The speaker *asserts* that the verbal process has occurred, is occurring, or is likely to occur. It is the most common of the moods.

Why talk of the speaker's role in all this? A person can willfully convey lies, distortion, etc., that are far from reality. The indicative mood is not a mood of the real in the sense of "actual." It is only real or declarative in the sense of what the speaker *asserts* to be real or declarative.

IRREAL MOOD

Volitional Mood

The VOLITIONAL MOOD imposes the will of the speaker on an entity being addressed. It is irreal, however, because the speaker's desire depends on whether the addressee will accede to the speaker's will. The speaker's will is thus not actual unless the addressee performs what the speaker desires. In anticipation of looking at Biblical Greek, we can talk about two different types of volitional moods, or *volitives:* 2d and 3d person volition.

2d Person Volition

SECOND PERSON VOLITION is better known among English speakers as the IMPERATIVE. The speaker wishes to impose his or her will on the grammatical 2d person. The order may be to one person or several people. The imperative commonly uses the dictionary form of the verb but no 2d person subject pronoun (see PRONOUN, p. 121), though it may occur.

Bow before the Procurator!

Sit here!

You, *stop* that!

English acrolect (the prestige variety of the language) also expresses the impera-tive by *you shall + verb*. By contrast, *you will + verb* expresses the future tense (see TENSE, p. 60) of the indicative mood. Few English speakers keep this distinction clear.[23]

> You **shall** *keep* the Sabbath! (= 2d person volition = imperative)
>
>> The speaker is imposing his or her will on the addressee. The addressee is expected to obey the order.
>
> You **will** *keep* the Sabbath. (= indicative mood)
>
>> The speaker is simply stating actuality.

3d Person Volition

In **3D PERSON VOLITION** the speaker wishes to impose his or her will on the grammatical 3d person, singular or plural.

> *May* YHWH *bless* you!
> *Let him pass!*
> *Long live Caesar!* (= *May Caesar live!*)
> *Let them enter* Jerusalem!

Nonvolitional Irreal Mood

The nonvolitional irreal mood is an expression of the speaker's will or attitude about a situation without imposing the will.

---

[23] As I mentioned in the introduction, within the halls of the academy, the commonest surround-ings I envision for this textbook, it is pedagogically useful to use English's acrolect, its *prestige* forms, while pointing out pertinent *colloquial* forms. The academy, on occasion, still expects the ac-rolect of its students.

Subjunctive Mood

The subjunctive mood commonly expresses a situation or condition that is not actual. It expresses an irreal *projection* of a situation or condition. The term *subjunctive* appears to reflect that this mood is commonly found in subordinate clauses, that is, clauses that are *subjoined* (see **DEPENDENT/SUBORDINATE**, p. 194, under **CLAUSE**). It is in such subjoined clauses that this mood frequently projects a particular situation. The subjunctive mood can, however, occur in independent clauses.

Those of you who have had languages such as Spanish, German, or Latin have had to learn paradigms of verbal forms known as the subjunctive. In English, the situation is far less complex, which accounts for a great deal of confusion for many English speakers in identifying the use of the subjunctive mood. English speakers, in fact, seem to be using it less and less. The following represent where we characteristically find the subjunctive.

➤ Clauses that begin with *if* and are a *projection* in the mind of the speaker are in the subjunctive mood.

If I *were* you, I would run. (= subjunctive mood)

                          subordinate clause
                          verb is subjunctive mood

    The verb follows *if* and expresses a projection in the mind of the speaker: here the speaker ("I") projects herself onto an addressee ("you").

If I *was* you, I would run. (= English basilect, not acrolect/"prestige")[24]

    This is, at best, basilect. At worst, it is incorrect grammar. It should not be used by the speaker to project herself on the addressee.

---

[24] As I mentioned in the introduction, within the halls of the academy, the commonest surroundings I envision for this textbook, it is pedagogically useful to use English's acrolect, its *prestige* forms, while pointing out pertinent *colloquial* forms. The academy, on occasion, still expects the acrolect of its students.

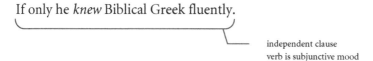

If only he *knew* Biblical Greek fluently.

independent clause
verb is subjunctive mood

The verb follows *if* and projects a condition concerning another: "he" doesn't know Greek fluently but the speaker projects that situation.

➤ Clauses that begin with *though* (= concessive, that is, a projection of conceding or acknowledging something) are often in the subjunctive mood.

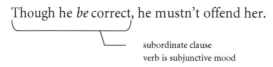

Though he *be* correct, he mustn't offend her.

subordinate clause
verb is subjunctive mood

➤ Clauses that *follow* a verb that expresses a wish, a demand, a doubt, a request, or a proposal are in the subjunctive mood. Here are some verbs that often govern clauses where English acrolect/"prestige" uses (or should use) the subjunctive: *wish, demand, request, command, suggest, prefer, ask, insist.*

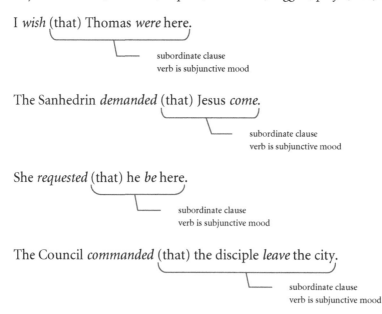

I *wish* (that) Thomas *were* here.

subordinate clause
verb is subjunctive mood

The Sanhedrin *demanded* (that) Jesus *come.*

subordinate clause
verb is subjunctive mood

She *requested* (that) he *be* here.

subordinate clause
verb is subjunctive mood

The Council *commanded* (that) the disciple *leave* the city.

subordinate clause
verb is subjunctive mood

➢ Clauses that follow the following constructions are in the subjunctive mood: *it is essential/important/necessary/vital* + (*that*).

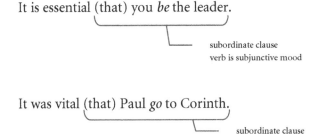

It is essential (that) you *be* the leader.

subordinate clause
verb is subjunctive mood

It was vital (that) Paul *go* to Corinth.

subordinate clause
verb is subjunctive mood

The form of the subjunctive is quite simple. The subjunctive does not change in form regardless of person (1st, 2d, 3d). With one prominent exception, the subjunctive form of most verbs is the dictionary form (= English infinitive without *to*). The exception is *be*, which uses *were* for the past.

FORM OF THE SUBJUNCTIVE		
(TO) BE		MOST OTHER VERBS: SAME AS INFINITIVE E.G., (TO) LIVE
PAST	PRESENT	PAST AND PRESENT
I *were*	I *be*	I *live*
you *were*	you *be*	you *live*
he, she, it *were*	he, she, it *be*	he, she, it *live*
we *were*	we *be*	we *live*
you *were*	you *be*	you *live*
they *were*	they *be*	they *live*

"Modals"

English also uses a variety of *modal auxiliaries* (*may, should, ought, can, might, must,* etc.), which we have called "modals." Rather than have special verb forms that express a variety of attitudes, English adds these "modals" into the clause along with a verb.

> Permission: conveys the speaker's permission for an entity to carry out a verbal process.

You *may feed* the children.

He *may live* on my holy hill.

> Obligation: conveys what the speaker or addressee considers necessary, an obligation.

You *should go* to Jerusalem.

This is what I *ought to do.*

> Capability: conveys the speaker or addressee's capability to perform a verbal process.

You *can leave* the prison now.

A stone *could kill* Stephen.

> Possibility: conveys the possibility of what the speaker or addressee says about a verbal process.

That event *might happen.*

Paul *might return* to Corinth.

> Necessity: conveys the necessity on the speaker or addressee to carry out a verbal process.

You *must return* to Corinth.

I *must return* to Corinth.

> Deliberation: conveys the speaker or addressee's deliberation on whether to carry out a verbal process. This is commonly found in question form.

Should we *attend* the feast in Jerusalem?

Should you *live* by the river?

BIBLICAL GREEK

We refer to the real mood in Biblical Greek as the INDICATIVE MOOD.

We shall place under the irreal moods Biblical Greek's IMPERATIVE, SUBJUNCTIVE, and OPTATIVE moods.

We thus have the following:

(1) real mood = indicative mood
(2) irreal mood
    (a) imperative mood
    (b) subjunctive mood
    (c) optative mood

REAL MOOD = INDICATIVE MOOD

Also known as the DECLARATIVE mood because it *declares,* the real or indicative mood in Biblical Greek routinely, but not exhaustively does the following:

➤ *asserts* (what is intended to be understood as) a fact (= declarative indicative)

    ὁ νόμος **κυριεύει** τοῦ ἀνθρώπου   The law *has power over* a person.

    the law   **it-has-power-over** the human   Romans 7:1

    • and, closely related, *probes* for information, often expecting an assertion in return:[25]

        σὺ **εἶ** ὁ βασιλεὺς τῶν Ἰουδαίων   *Are* you the king of the Jews?

        you **are-you** the king   of(-the) Jews   Matthew 27:11

➤ *asserts* a condition (= conditional indicative):

    εἰ **ἔστιν** σῶμα ψυχικόν ἔστιν καὶ πνευματικόν   If *there is* a physical body,

    if **it-is** body physical it-is also spiritual   there is also a spiritual one.

                                                 1 Corinthians 15:44

---

[25] Some grammars label this function separately as an INTERROGATIVE INDICATIVE. I have not treated it as an entirely separate function because it is simply the first turned into a question. The realm of meaning or of semantics here is arguably the same whether one is asserting or asking.

The indicative conveys a verbal process that meshes with the speaker's perception of reality and his or her intent to have the hearer understand reality accordingly. The speaker makes an *assertion* about the verbal process. It is the most common of the Biblical Greek moods.

Why talk of the speaker's role in all this? A person can willfully convey lies, distortions, etc., that are far from reality. The indicative mood is not a mood of the real in the sense of "actual." It is only real or declarative in the sense of what the speaker *asserts* to be real or declarative.

IRREAL MOOD

Imperative Mood

The **IMPERATIVE MOOD** imposes the will of the speaker on an entity. It is irreal because the speaker's desire depends on whether the addressee will accede to the speaker's will. The speaker's will is thus not actual unless the addressee does what the speaker desires. Biblical Greek expresses the imperative mood in the 2d and 3d persons. Negative imperatives or **PROHIBITIONS** are routinely formed by μή (or related form) placed before the imperative, most commonly the *present "tense"-form* imperative.

Our view is that Biblical Greek's verbal system is fundamentally aspectual (see the chapter **TENSE AND ASPECT**, p. 60). The aorist "tense"-form imperative, as *perfective* aspect, conveys the verbal process as an undivided *whole* or *totality,* without dividing up the internal temporal structure needed to accomplish it. The present "tense"-form imperative, as *imperfective* aspect, conveys the verbal process from the *inside,* considering the *process,* that is, the internal temporal structure needed to achieve it.

Imperative 2d Person

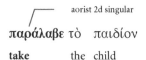

παράλαβε τὸ παιδίον
take   the child

Take the child.

Matthew 2:13

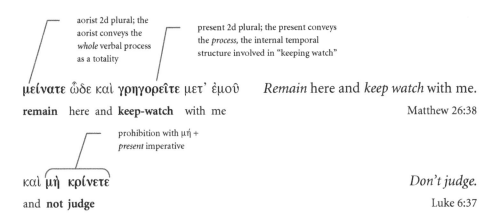

μείνατε ὧδε καὶ **γρηγορεῖτε** μετ' ἐμοῦ

remain here and **keep-watch** with me

Remain here and *keep watch* with me.

Matthew 26:38

prohibition with μή +
present imperative

καὶ **μὴ κρίνετε**

and **not judge**

Don't judge.

Luke 6:37

The last example leads to an important observation. When Biblical Greek wishes to prohibit, using μή plus the aorist "tense"-form, it does *not* use an aorist *imperative*. The language, rather, uses μή plus an aorist *subjunctive* (see below, PROHIBITIVE SUBJUNCTIVE, p. 93).

Imperative 3d Person

With Biblical Greek's 3d person imperative, we encounter a bit of disparity in how English routinely translates it. English conveys the 3d person imperative commonly in the form of the *permissive* or the *jussive:* "*Let* him/her *go, stand, stay,* etc." (See the chapter TRANSLATION, p. 20, which discusses FORM and MEANING.) This English phenomenon sounds less direct to an English speaker. Biblical Greek's 3d person imperative is, however, every bit as direct as its 2d person imperative.

present 3d singular

ὁ ἔχων ὦτα **ἀκουέτω**

the one-having ears **hear**

Hear, you with ears.

(or: *Let* the one with ears *hear*.)

Matthew 11:15

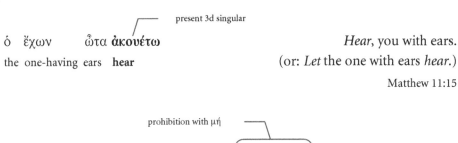

prohibition with μή

ὃ οὖν ὁ θεὸς συνέζευξεν ἄνθρωπος **μὴ χωριζέτω**

what thus the God he-joined person **not separate**

What God has joined,

no person *must separate.*

Mark 10:9

Subjunctive Mood

In Biblical Greek the subjunctive mood expresses a situation or condition that is not actual. It expresses an irreal *projection* of a situation or condition. The term *subjunctive* appears to reflect that this mood is regularly found in dependent/subordinate clauses, that is, clauses that are *subjoined* (see DEPENDENT/SUBORDINATE, p. 194, under CLAUSE). The subjunctive mood can, however, occur in independent clauses. We shall, in fact, look at some common functions of the subjunctive in independent and dependent/subordinate clauses respectively.

Independent Clause

I shall mention three of the more common functions of the subjunctive mood in independent clauses.

Imperatival (or Hortative) Subjunctive

We read above that Biblical Greek's imperative mood operates on the 2d and 3d persons. Biblical Greek uses the subjunctive to project the will of the speaker onto the 1st person, singular and plural: "let me . . . , I must . . . , let us . . . ," etc.

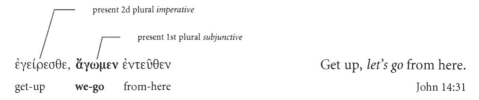

ἐγείρεσθε,	**ἄγωμεν**	ἐντεῦθεν	Get up, *let's go* from here.
get-up	**we-go**	from-here	John 14:31

This function can be used in a question, which some grammars treat separately and call the DELIBERATIVE SUBJUNCTIVE. Although we can identify different shades of meaning within this "questioning" form, grammars generally agree that the so-called deliberative subjunctive is merely "the interrogative form of the hortatory."[26]

---

[26] Nigel Turner, *Syntax* (vol. 3 of James Hope Moulton, *A Grammar of New Testament Greek;* Edinburgh: T& T Clark, 1963), 98.

τὸν βασιλέα ὑμῶν **σταυρώσω**

the king of-you **I-crucify**

Should I crucify your king?

John 19:15

Prohibitive Subjunctive

The negative adverb μή plus an *aorist* subjunctive can be used by Biblical Greek to forbid the totality of a verbal process and, depending on context or textual environment, can forbid the *start* of one, that is, "*Never* (do something)." Biblical Greek does *not* use μή plus an aorist *imperative*. If it wishes to prohibit an aorist verbal process, Biblical Greek uses the prohibitive (aorist) subjunctive.

μὴ φονεύσῃς μὴ κλέψῃς

not you-murder not you-steal

Never murder, never steal!

Luke 18:20

Emphatic (or Marked) Negation Subjunctive

Biblical Greek can express strong negation with οὐ μή plus, most commonly, the *aorist* subjunctive.

ἰῶτα ἓν ἢ μία κεραία **οὐ μὴ παρέλθῃ**

iota one or single stroke **not not it-disappears**

Not an iota or single letter stroke will ever disappear!

Matthew 5:18

Dependent/Subordinate Clause

Here are a few of the many different occurrences of the subjunctive mood in dependent/subordinate clauses.

ἵνα + Subjunctive

This structure is the most common use of the subjunctive in dependent/subordinate clauses. The conjunction ἵνα initiates the clause. Such a clause can convey diverse *semantic* connections (purpose, result, etc.) and play different syntactic roles (subject, complement, etc.).

➢ Purpose: here the spotlight is on the *purpose* or *intention* of the verbal process conveyed by the verb in the *main* clause (see INDEPENDENT AND MAIN under the chapter on CLAUSE, p. 193). You will find that many call such clauses TELIC or FINAL clauses. In addition to ἵνα, Biblical Greek uses the conjunction ὅπως for this semantic connection.

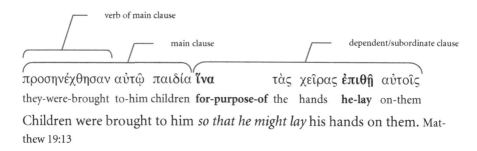

προσηνέχθησαν αὐτῷ παιδία **ἵνα** τὰς χεῖρας **ἐπιθῇ** αὐτοῖς
they-were-brought to-him children **for-purpose-of** the hands **he-lay** on-them

Children were brought to him *so that he might lay* his hands on them. Matthew 19:13

➤ Result: here the focus is on the *result* accomplished by the verbal process that the verb in the *main* clause conveys.

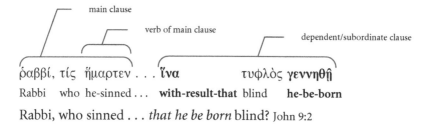

ῥαββί, τίς ἥμαρτεν . . . **ἵνα** τυφλὸς **γεννηθῇ**
Rabbi who he-sinned . . . **with-result-that** blind **he-be-born**

Rabbi, who sinned . . . *that he be born* blind? John 9:2

➤ Syntactic Constituent: here the entire ἵνα-initiated clause functions as a syntactic constituent or component within a larger clausal structure: subject, complement, etc.

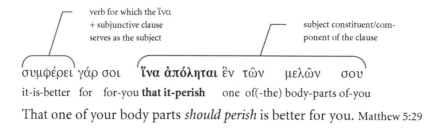

συμφέρει γάρ σοι **ἵνα ἀπόληται** ἓν τῶν μελῶν σου
it-is-better for for-you **that it-perish** one of(-the) body-parts of-you

That one of your body parts *should perish* is better for you. Matthew 5:29

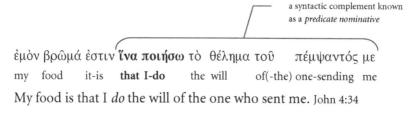

ἐμὸν βρῶμά ἐστιν **ἵνα ποιήσω** τὸ θέλημα τοῦ πέμψαντός με
my food it-is **that I-do** the will of(-the) one-sending me

My food is that I *do* the will of the one who sent me. John 4:34

Conditional Clause

Biblical Greek, like many languages, has a complex array of factors to consider in conditional-clause structures. This is not the place to rehearse them. We want, rather, to remind ourselves that we are talking about what we in English understand simply as the *if–then* structure: "*If* (something), *then* (something)." The *if* portion is known as the PROTASIS. It is a dependent/subordinate clause and conveys the condition. The *then* portion is the APODOSIS, usually a main clause, which conveys the consequence of the condition.

It is easy to see how articulating a condition can be a *projection*—and thus the world of the subjunctive. Not all conditional clauses use the subjunctive. We should likely understand that those that use the subjunctive are more hypothetical than those that use, for example, the indicative mood.

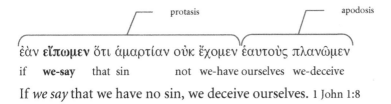

protasis   apodosis

ἐὰν **εἴπωμεν** ὅτι ἁμαρτίαν οὐκ ἔχομεν ἑαυτοὺς πλανῶμεν

if **we-say** that sin   not we-have ourselves we-deceive

If *we say* that we have no sin, we deceive ourselves. 1 John 1:8

Relative Clause

The subjunctive may occur in a *relative* clause after either the definite or indefinite relative pronoun (see **DEFINITE AND INDEFINITE RELATIVE PRONOUN**, p. 156) and where the clause expresses an irreal projection of a situation. This projection is routinely expressed in the clause by ἄν/ἐάν.

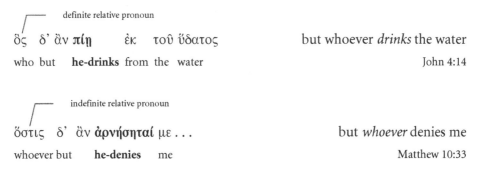

definite relative pronoun

ὃς δ᾽ ἂν **πίῃ** ἐκ τοῦ ὕδατος   but whoever *drinks* the water

who but **he-drinks** from the water   John 4:14

indefinite relative pronoun

ὅστις δ᾽ ἂν **ἀρνήσηταί** με . . .   but *whoever* denies me

whoever but **he-denies** me   Matthew 10:33

Optative Mood

By the time the first century C.E. arrived, the optative mood had been dying a slow death. We do not know all the reasons for its decline. No small factor, though, was likely the challenge it presented to the myriad of people who were learning Greek as a second language in the centuries after Alexander the Great. A great hurdle, no doubt, was sorting out precisely how the optative differed from the closely related subjunctive. Increasingly, the subjunctive, in part, took on the roles that the dying optative had played. Features of language easily become fuzzy. Observe, for example, how very few native English speakers know the original distinction between *will* and *shall*.

Like the subjunctive, the optative in Biblical Greek expresses an irreal *projection* of a situation or condition. It differs from the subjunctive, however, by appearing to express a projection that is more contingent. It is *less* real, or *more* irreal, than the subjunctive.

Its overall frequency in Biblical Greek is somewhat skewed. About a fourth of all occurrences are found in one of Paul's set phrases, μὴ γένοιτο *May it never happen/be so!*

Like the subjunctive, we can look at the optative in independent and dependent/subordinate clauses.

Independent Clause

Voluntative Optative

The **VOLUNTATIVE** or **VOLITIVE OPTATIVE** expresses a wishful request. We find it in prayerful language, where it likely conveys polite and tactful entreaty. We also find it in set phrases, such as μὴ γένοιτο, where, rather than a mere request, it has become a forceful and strong expression of detestation.

μὴ γένοιτο	*May* it never *happen!*
not **it-happen**	Romans 3:6

γένοιτό μοι κατὰ τὸ ῥῆμά σου   *May it be done* to me as you've said.

it-happen to-me according-to the word of-you   Luke 1:38

Potential Optative

This expresses what would or might be possible. In Biblical Greek it occurs with the particle ἄν, which conveys contingency.

εὐξαίμην ἂν τῷ θεῷ   I *would wish* to God

I-would-wish to(-the) God   Acts 26:29

τί ἂν θέλοι ὁ σπερμολόγος οὗτος λέγειν   What *would* this parroting,

what **he-would-wish** the seed-picker this say   cliché-speaker *wish* to say?

    Acts 17:18

Dependent/Subordinate Clause

Conditional Optative

As we read a few pages back, we are here talking about the English *if–then* structure: "*If* (something), *then* (something)." The *if* portion is known as the PROTASIS. It is a dependent/subordinate clause and conveys the condition. The *then* portion is the APODOSIS, usually a main clause, which conveys the consequence of the condition.

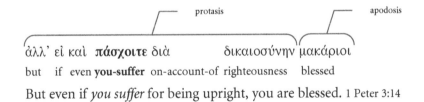

ἀλλ’ εἰ καὶ **πάσχοιτε** διὰ δικαιοσύνην μακάριοι

but if even **you-suffer** on-account-of righteousness blessed

But even if *you suffer* for being upright, you are blessed. 1 Peter 3:14

VOICE

VOICE refers either to (1) a fundamental part in producing sound (see SOUND PRODUCTION, p. 7) or (2) a relationship between the grammatical subject, the verb, and adverbials. This chapter focuses solely on the latter meaning.

We need to understand the *syntactic* notions of SUBJECT (see SUBJECT, p. 198) and DIRECT OBJECT (see DIRECT OBJECT ACCUSATIVE, p. 46, under the chapter on CASE) and the semantic roles of AGENT–PATIENT, SENSER–PHENOMENON, and BENEFICIARY (see SEMANTICS: PROCESSES, ROLES, AND CIRCUMSTANCES, p. 203). Our discussion here uses two terms that embrace or subsume the more specific terms of agent–patient or senser–phenomenon, etc.

- INITIATOR: the semantic concept referring to an entity responsible for a process

- RECEPTOR: the semantic concept referring to the entity receiving a process[27]

In a clause, we may find a word or word grouping that is the grammatical *subject* as well as the semantic *initiator*. The *subject* and *initiator* labels refer to that same word or word grouping from two different perspectives. One is from the perspective of *syntax,* the other from *semantic roles.* Sometimes we find a word or word grouping that is the grammatical *direct object* as well as the semantic *receptor.* Subject, direct object, initiator, and receptor are important in understanding voice.

Below we shall be learning about the (1) active, (2) passive, (3) reflexive, and (4) middle voices. The last two, reflexive and middle, require special comment. Many languages, including Biblical Greek, have special verbal forms to express the middle voice. In those languages, the middle forms routinely express a wide range of

---

[27] Though these terms are not both hers, I am indebted to the work of Suzanne Kemmer for the notion of using such overarching terms. Additionally, my discussion of the middle voice is greatly influenced by her. See Suzanne Kemmer, *The Middle Voice* (Typological Studies in Language 23; Amsterdam and Philadelphia: John Benjamins, 1993).

verbal processes, *one* of which is something we can call *reflexive*. For Biblical Greek, we shall call the voice the *middle(–reflexive)*. For English, we shall separate these two conceptually close voices, primarily to help us see their differences.

English conveys both a reflexive and a middle. The reflexive is *clearly* expressed. A particular structure/syntax expresses it. The middle, less clearly, does *not* regularly have a special structure or have special verbal forms. Often it can look like the active voice. That creates a hurdle for us in English. The hurdle is substantial enough that it has produced an incorrect notion of DEPONENT VERBS among Biblical Greek grammarians. More about that later (see EXCURSUS: SO-CALLED "DEPONENT" VERBS, p. 106).

ENGLISH

Within English, we can talk about four voices: (1) active, (2) passive, (3) reflexive, and (4) middle. I am treating reflexive and middle separately, though they are, as I noted above, closely and conceptually related—so closely that Biblical Greek's middle voice subsumes both concepts.

ACTIVE VOICE

The active voice is expressed when the grammatical subject is also the semantic initiator. The subject performs the verb's process. Further, the verbal process initiated by the initiator has minimal impact back toward the initiator. We shall return to this later under the middle voice.

Look at an example where the verb is *intransitive* (does not govern a direct object).

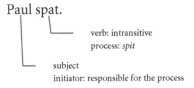

Paul spat.

      verb: intransitive
      process: *spit*

  subject
  initiator: responsible for the process

Now consider an example where the verb is *transitive* (governs a direct object).

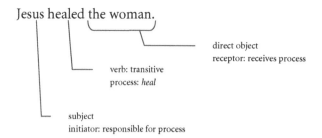

When the verb is transitive and we thus have a direct object, the direct object is also the semantic receptor.

➢ The active voice, then, is expressed when

the subject is the initiator of a verbal process that has minimal impact back on the initiator (and, if present, the direct object is the receptor).

PASSIVE VOICE

The passive voice is expressed when the grammatical subject is also the semantic receptor. The subject receives the verb's process. Further, an initiator is in mind, whether explicitly expressed or not.

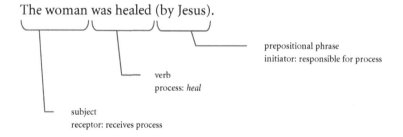

➢ The passive voice, then, is expressed when

the subject is the receptor and an initiator is in mind, whether explicit or implicit.

REFLEXIVE VOICE

The reflexive voice is expressed when the grammatical subject is the semantic initiator and receptor. The subject both performs and receives the verb's process.

The initiator carries out a verbal process on itself just as it would on another entity. In English, a reflexive pronoun (a pronoun that refers back to the subject) functions as a direct object.

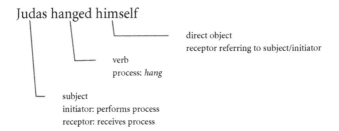

Judas hanged himself

direct object
receptor referring to subject/initiator

verb
process: *hang*

subject
initiator: performs process
receptor: receives process

➢ The reflexive voice, then, is expressed when

the subject is both the semantic initiator and receptor and a reflexive pronoun stands as a direct object and refers to the subject.

MIDDLE VOICE

The middle voice is not without its hurdles in arriving at a clear understanding. English speakers encounter such barriers because, unlike Biblical Greek, for example, English does *not* offer a special form of the verb when expressing the middle voice. The middle voice in English, without special verbal forms, often looks similar to the active voice. A *conceptual* difference, however, lies at the heart of understanding the middle from the other voices. Let's start by contrasting the middle with the reflexive. They are closely related.

For the reflexive, the subject both performs and receives the verb's process. The initiator, in the reflexive, carries out a verbal process on itself just as it would on another entity.

The middle voice, though, involves a *closer fusion* between the initiator and receptor than a corresponding reflexive. The two semantic roles of initiator and receptor are participants in a more holistic verbal process than in the reflexive.

Here is a way to conceptualize the difference.[28]

---

[28] The idea of the conceptualization is from Kemmer, *The Middle Voice,* p. 71.

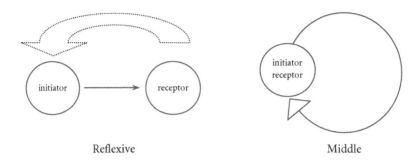

Reflexive   Middle

Here are some sample clauses to illustrate the difference.

(1) Herod shaved himself. =   reflexive

(2) Herod shaved.   =   middle

(3) The tablet broke.   =   middle

(4) Paul bowed.   =   middle

(5) Felix strolled.   =   middle

(6) Mary pondered.   =   middle

Example 1 is reflexive. The syntactic subject and semantic initiator, *Herod*, is here carrying out a verbal process, 'shave', onto a syntactic direct object and semantic receptor, which is a reflexive pronoun. Herod is carrying out the verbal process just as he would on *any* entity. The initiator is here acting on a receptor, which happens to refer back to and have an impact on the initiator.

Example 2 is a middle voice GROOMING expression. Grooming is a common middle-voice phenomenon. *Herod shaved* is conceptually a closer fusion of the initiator and receptor than the reflexive counterpart, example 1. Examples 1 and 2 share the phenomenon that an initiator is making an impact on itself, but they are different because example 2 conveys a more holistic verbal process than in the reflexive. Additionally, *Herod shaved* is not the active voice, though it may seem similar to it. The verbal process involved in the active voice has *minimal* impact back onto an initiator. In the active voice expression, *Herod spat*, the verbal process of 'spit' is not conveying an impact back onto *Herod*, the initiator. But in *Herod shaved*, the process of 'shave' *impacts* the initiator, *Herod*.

Example 3 represents a large group within the middle voice we can label SPON-TANEOUS EVENT.[29] These are other examples: *The food burnt; The mountain eroded; The bubble burst; The cloud vanished; The race began; The water shimmered.* With this group of middle constructions we can clearly envision the close fusion of initiator and receptor conceptualized by a circular arrow coming back on itself.

Examples 4 and 5 represent another large group centered around MOTION. *Paul bowed* is an example of *nonspatial* movement, movement without traveling spatially. *Felix strolled* is *spatial* movement, traveling spatially. As with all middles, the initiator and receptor enjoy a close fusion. By bowing, Paul is both initiator and receptor. By strolling, Felix, too, is both initiator and receptor.

Mary pondered, example 6, expresses COGNITION, another sphere of the middle voice. The process of mulling over or pondering is one where Mary is both initiator and receptor.

Notice something important. All the middle-voice examples above are intransitive (the verb does *not* take a direct object). Their intransitivity, along with the close fusion of initiator and receptor, places them squarely within the middle voice. But what happens when an expression has a verb from one of the middle-voice spheres (cognition, movement, spontaneous event, etc.) and has transitivity (a direct object is governed by a verb)? The principle to keep in mind is, again, that the middle expresses a *close fusion* of the initiator and receptor. If transitivity erodes that fusion significantly, we are no longer encountering the middle. *Mary pondered,* for example, could become *Mary pondered these things.* We could well understand *Mary pondered these things* as the active voice; *Mary,* the initiator, is not closely fused with the receptor, *these things.* Biblical Greek, because its verbs *explicitly* show three distinct voices, assists us more clearly. In Luke 2:19, where Mary is "pondering these things," Biblical Greek uses the active voice there. It does not envision, in that particular text, a close fusion of initiator and receptor.

---

[29] The term is from Kemmer, *The Middle Voice,* p. 19 and passim.

It is the *relative distinguishability of initiator and receptor* that separates the middle from the reflexive. The more *in*distinguishable the initiator and receptor, the *closer* we are to the middle voice, and thus *further* from the reflexive. With middle and reflexive bundled together (as in Biblical Greek) as compared with the active and passive, the initiator of the middle–reflexive is impacted more by a verbal process than is the case in the active and passive voices.

➢ The middle voice, then, is expressed when

the subject is both the semantic initiator and receptor, but middle voice involves a *closer fusion* between the initiator and receptor than a corresponding reflexive. The two semantic roles of initiator and receptor are participants in a more holistic verbal process than in the reflexive.

BIBLICAL GREEK

Whereas in English we spoke of four voices, the Biblical Greek verbal system shows *three* voices: (1) active, (2) passive, and (3) middle(–reflexive).

ACTIVE VOICE

The active voice, as I said above, is expressed when the grammatical subject is also the semantic initiator. The subject performs the verb's process. Further, the verbal process initiated by the initiator has minimal impact back toward the initiator.

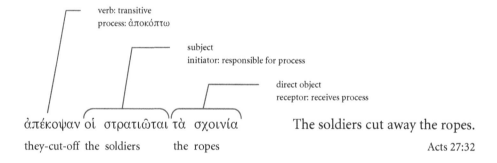

verb: transitive
process: ἀποκόπτω

subject
initiator: responsible for process

direct object
receptor: receives process

ἀπέκοψαν οἱ στρατιῶται τὰ σχοινία   The soldiers cut away the ropes.
they-cut-off the soldiers   the ropes   Acts 27:32

PASSIVE VOICE

The passive voice is expressed when the grammatical subject is also the semantic receptor. The subject receives the verb's process. Further, an initiator is in mind, whether explicitly expressed or not.

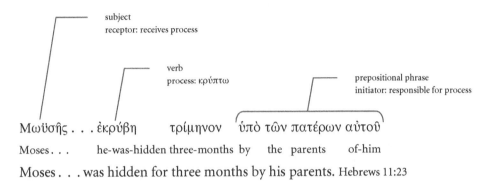

Μωϋσῆς . . . ἐκρύβη   τρίμηνον   ὑπὸ τῶν πατέρων αὐτοῦ

Moses . . .   he-was-hidden three-months by   the   parents   of-him

Moses . . . was hidden for three months by his parents. Hebrews 11:23

MIDDLE(–REFLEXIVE) VOICE

In Biblical Greek one verbal form conveys what is best called the middle(–reflexive). The initiator of a middle(–reflexive) verbal process is impacted more by the verb's process than is the case in the active and passive voices.

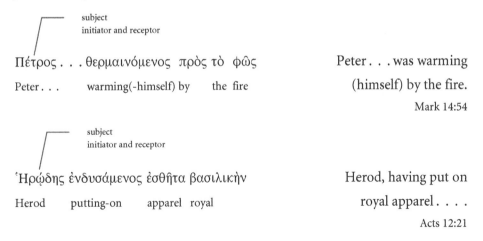

Πέτρος . . . θερμαινόμενος πρὸς τὸ φῶς

Peter . . .   warming(-himself) by   the fire

Peter . . . was warming (himself) by the fire.

Mark 14:54

Ἡρῴδης ἐνδυσάμενος ἐσθῆτα βασιλικὴν

Herod   putting-on   apparel royal

Herod, having put on royal apparel. . . .

Acts 12:21

As these examples show, the middle(–reflexive) voice conveys a close fusion of the initiator and the receptor.

105

Excursus: So-Called "Deponent" Verbs

Many, if not most, Biblical Greek grammars use the term *deponent verb* to refer to verbs they claim to be active in *meaning* but middle(–reflexive) or passive in *form*. Such verbs, in fact, do not appear in an active form. They are said to have "*put aside* [their active form]" (Latin *depono* "lay aside").

The meaning of so-called deponent verbs is regularly *middle* voice, not active. No small role in this confusion is that analysts have not always recognized that what they think is an active verbal process is, in reality, a middle process. We should not expect a truly middle verbal process to have an active form because it is *not* active, it is middle. These are not verbs that have laid aside an active form; they are verbs that convey middle verbal processes clothed appropriately with a middle form. Here are some examples:

- ἅλλομαι *leap*, πορεύομαι *travel* = spatial motion middle

- ἔρχομαι *appear*, γίνομαι *become* = spontaneous event middle

That some so-called deponents are passive in form is likely a testimony to a breakdown in the distinction between middle and passive voices among Greek users after the classical period.[30] We cannot know for sure why this happened. Passive forms, though, are more regular. Using a reflexive pronoun with active verbs might have been seen as more explicit for conveying certain middle verbal processes. Lastly, middles and passives in some forms are not dissimilar. A passive form, in time, then, would also come to convey, in instances, the middle voice. An example of this might be ἀπεκρίθην *I answered* (a middle phenomenon cast in the clothes of a passive).

---

[30] Chrys C. Caragounis, *The Development of Greek and the New Testament: Morphology, Syntax, Phonology, and Textual Transmission* (Wissenschaftliche Untersuchungen zum Neuen Testament 167; Tübingen: Mohr Siebeck, 2004), 152.

ARTICLE

An ARTICLE, in part, *identifies*. While this is likely not a most inclusive definition, to talk of the article as something that identifies gives us an understanding that can embrace its function in English and its use in Biblical Greek.

ENGLISH

In English the article identifies in that it commonly stipulates whether a nominal is *unspecified* or *specified*. We have two primary articles. One we call INDEFINITE. The other we call DEFINITE.

INDEFINITE ARTICLE

An indefinite article is placed before a nominal when it does *not* specify a particular person, animal, place, thing, event, or idea.

➢ English places an *a* before a word that begins with a consonantal sound.

Peter saw *a* relative.

                         not a specified relative

➢ English places an ***an*** before a word that begins with a vowel sound.

Herod looked at *an* altar.

                         not a specified altar

DEFINITE ARTICLE

English has one definite article, *the*.

The definite article usually specifies that a nominal is PARTICULAR—a particular person, animal, place, thing, event, or idea. It also can specify that the nominal is CATEGORICAL, that is, when it is representative of a *category* of person, animal, place, thing, event, or idea.

➢ Particular

Herod looked at *the* altar.

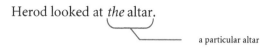

a particular altar

➢ Categorical

The Roman world had *the* tax collector.

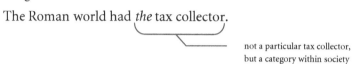

not a particular tax collector,
but a category within society

We identify a definite article as particular or categorical from the text surrounding it, that is, from the *textual environment* or *textual context*.

BIBLICAL GREEK

Biblical Greek does not have an indefinite article. We, therefore, have little need to talk of indefinite and definite articles, as we do for English. For Biblical Greek, we may talk simply of the *article*.

Here is a table of the forms of the article.

	2d Declension masculine	1st Declension feminine	2d Declension neuter
nominative sg	ὁ	ἡ	τό
accusative sg	τόν	τήν	τό
genitive sg	τοῦ	τῆς	τοῦ
dative sg	τῷ	τῇ	τῷ
nominative pl	οἱ	αἱ	τά
accusative pl	τούς	τάς	τά
genitive pl	τῶν	τῶν	τῶν
dative pl	τοῖς	ταῖς	τοῖς

Figure 16: Forms of the Biblical Greek Article

Down along the left side you see each *case* and *number*, whether singular (sg) or plural (pl). Along the top you see *gender*, whether masculine, feminine, or neuter.

108

You also confront the word *declension* (see DECLENSION, p. 29). The form of words can change; this is known as INFLECTION. For example, *man* can become *men*. Biblical Greek has three inflectional patterns. Each pattern is known as a DECLENSION. The table shows that the masculine and neuter genders follow the second declension whereas the feminine follows the first.

Nailing down the Biblical Greek article exhaustively into simple, clear functions is not an easy task. The following chart, loosely adapted from D. A. Carson,[31] offers some of the more common roles—*but not all*—when the article is used and not used. When a noun/nominal has an article, it is ARTHROUS/ARTICULAR; when no article is present, it is ANARTHROUS.

Arthrous/Articular (with article)			Particular	Categorical	Function & Clarification
			similar	similar	
Anarthrous (with*out*) article	Indefinite		Individual	Qualitative	

Figure 17: Meanings of Arthrous/Articular and Anarthrous Nominals

ARTHROUS/ARTICULAR NOMINALS

The Biblical Greek article identifies in that when the nominal is articular, the nominal can denote something PARTICULAR—a particular person, animal, place, thing, event, or idea. The articular nominal can also denote that it is representative of a CATEGORY of person, animal, place, thing, event, or idea. In these first two, we see some crossover with English. Finally, from figure 17 above, the articular nominal is used for particular FUNCTIONS and CLARIFICATION. Here are a few examples. (1) We can see that an adjective clearly functions as an adjective to modify an articular nominal when the adjective is also articular. (2) An articular nominal can refer back to a previously mentioned word or phrase, whether that

---

[31] D. A. Carson, *Exegetical Fallacies* (2d ed.; Grand Rapids, Mich.: Baker Books; Carlisle, England: Paternoster, 1996), 79.

word or phrase was originally articular or anarthrous. This is known as *anaphora* (Greek ἀναφέρειν *to bring back*). (3) In many clauses without a verb or with the verb εἰμί *to be*, the subject commonly has an articular nominal while the predicate does not. This can clarify the subject from the predicate (but it is not a hard-and-fast rule!).

➢ Particular

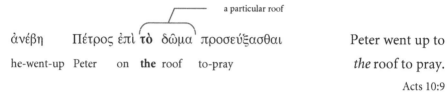

						Peter went up to
ἀνέβη	Πέτρος	ἐπὶ	**τὸ**	δῶμα	προσεύξασθαι	*the* roof to pray.
he-went-up	Peter	on	**the**	roof	to-pray	

Acts 10:9

➢ Categorical

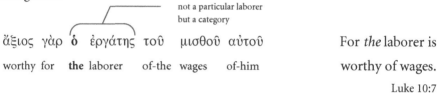

						For *the* laborer is
ἄξιος	γὰρ	**ὁ**	ἐργάτης	τοῦ	μισθοῦ αὐτοῦ	worthy of wages.
worthy	for	**the**	laborer	of-the	wages of-him	

Luke 10:7

➢ Function and Clarification

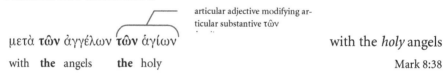

				with the *holy* angels
μετὰ	**τῶν** ἀγγέλων	**τῶν** ἁγίων		Mark 8:38
with	**the** angels	**the** holy		

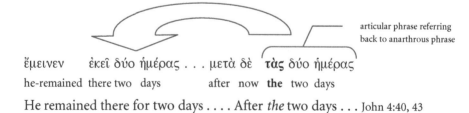

ἔμεινεν	ἐκεῖ δύο ἡμέρας . . .	μετὰ δὲ	**τὰς** δύο ἡμέρας	
he-remained	there two days	after now	**the** two days	

He remained there for two days . . . . After *the* two days . . . John 4:40, 43

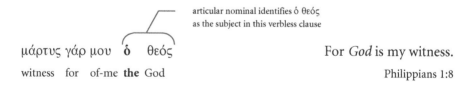

				For *God* is my witness.
μάρτυς	γάρ μου	**ὁ**	θεός	Philippians 1:8
witness	for of-me	**the**	God	

110

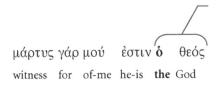

articular nominal identifies
ὁ θεός as the subject in this
verbal clause with εἰμί

μάρτυς γάρ μού ἐστιν **ὁ** θεός   For *God* is my witness.

witness for of-me he-is **the** God   Romans 1:9

ANARTHROUS NOMINALS

A nominal that does not have an article, that is, when it is anarthrous, can refer to something INDEFINITE, quite like English's use of the indefinite article. Anarthrous nominals can specify INDIVIDUAL persons, animals, places, things, events, or ideas. This use focuses on individual identity, often something already marked out or otherwise known. The QUALITATIVE function of anarthrous nominals highlights the essence, the nature, the quality of an item.

Figure 17 above shows that the articular nominal's *particular* and *categorical* functions are somewhat similar to the anarthrous's *individual* and *qualitative* functions respectively. Focusing on a *particular* item is similar to focusing on an *individual* item. Referring to *category* is not too dissimilar from referring to a *quality* of an item. It is, at the end of the day, textual environment or context that determines the function of articular or anarthrous nominals.

➢ Indefinite

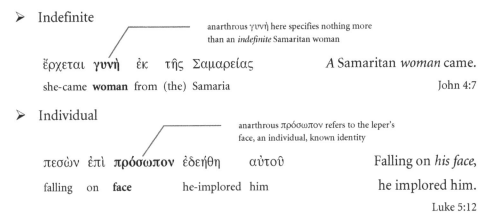

anarthrous γυνή here specifies nothing more
than an *indefinite* Samaritan woman

ἔρχεται **γυνὴ** ἐκ τῆς Σαμαρείας   *A* Samaritan *woman* came.

she-came **woman** from (the) Samaria   John 4:7

➢ Individual

anarthrous πρόσωπον refers to the leper's
face, an individual, known identity

πεσὼν ἐπὶ **πρόσωπον** ἐδεήθη αὐτοῦ   Falling on *his face*,

falling on **face**   he-implored him   he implored him.

                                                  Luke 5:12

anarthrous γυναικὸς refers to the already
known individual, the Samaritan woman

μετὰ **γυναικὸς** ἐλάλει

With *a/the woman* he was speaking.

with **woman** he-was-speaking

John 4:27

➤ Qualitative

the qualities of *grace* and *truth*

πλήρης **χάριτος** καὶ **ἀληθείας**

full of *grace* and *truth*

full **of-grace** and **of-truth**

John 1:14

112

CONJUNCTION

A CONJUNCTION is a word that links words, phrases, and clauses. We speak of two types of conjunctions: COORDINATING and SUBORDINATING.

➢ Coordinating conjunctions
Coordinate conjunctions join words, phrases, and clauses that are equal, connecting elements of equal status.

➢ Subordinating conjunctions
Subordinate conjunctions join DEPENDENT/SUBORDINATE clauses to main clauses (see CLAUSE, p. 193). A clause that does not stand on its own and must be linked to a main clause is a dependent or subordinate clause. The terms *dependent* and *subordinate* are quite synonymous.

CONJUNCTION OR PREPOSITION?

Some conjunctions also function as prepositions. When the word in question introduces a *clause,* the word is functioning as a *conjunction.* When the word does *not* introduce a clause, the word is functioning as a *preposition.* You will find examples below under the English and Biblical Greek sections.

ENGLISH

COORDINATING CONJUNCTIONS

The primary coordinating conjunctions in English are *and, but,* and *or.*

➢ Words

heaven *and* earth

➢ Phrases

in the city *but* outside the house

➢ Clauses

Paul could go to Rome, *or* he could go to Corinth.

SUBORDINATING CONJUNCTIONS

Some primary subordinating conjunctions in English are *because, if, although, unless, while,* and *that.*

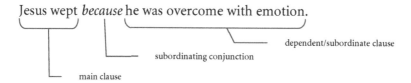

CONJUNCTION OR PREPOSITION?

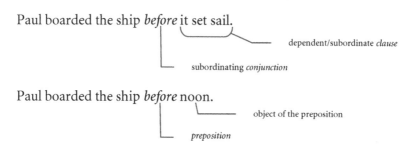

BIBLICAL GREEK

COORDINATING CONJUNCTIONS

Some of the primary coordinating conjunctions in Biblical Greek are καί, δέ, ἀλλά, γάρ, ἤ, and μέν . . . δέ.

➤ Words

χρυσὸν **καὶ** λίβανον	**καὶ** σμύρναν	gold, incense, *and* myrrh	
gold **and** frankincense	**and** myrrh	Matthew 2:11	

➤ Phrases

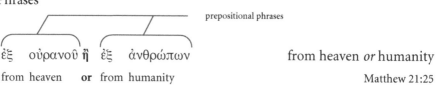

from heaven *or* humanity

Matthew 21:25

114

➢ Clauses

ὁ	**μὲν**	θερισμὸς πολύς	οἱ	**δὲ**	ἐργάται	ὀλίγοι
the	**on-one-hand**	harvest plentiful	the	**on-the-other**	laborers	few

(On the one hand) the harvest is plentiful, *but (on the other)* the laborers are few. Matthew 9:37

SUBORDINATING CONJUNCTIONS

Some of the primary subordinating conjunctions in Biblical Greek are γάρ, ὅτι, ὡς, εἰ, and καθώς.

CONJUNCTION OR PREPOSITION?

As in English, be careful not to confuse when a form is functioning as a conjunction or a preposition.

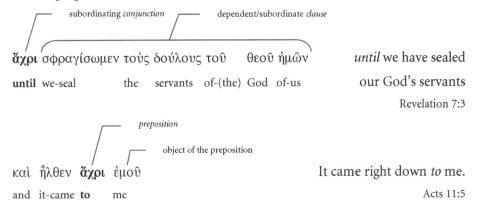

until we have sealed
our God's servants
Revelation 7:3

It came right down *to* me.
Acts 11:5

A SAMPLING OF THE SEMANTIC CONNECTIONS OF SOME CONJUNCTIONS

Temporal or Chronological Conjunctions

ἄχρι	until
ἕως	until, while
ὅταν	when, whenever
ὅτε	when, while, as long as, at which time
ὡς	as long as, when

Logical Conjunctions

Continuative

δέ	and, now, then, so
καί	and, also
οὖν	then, now (particularly in John: 3:25, 4:6, 28, etc.)

Contrast

ἀλλά	but, rather, on the contrary
δέ	but, rather, to the contrary
ἤ . . . ἤ	either . . . or
καί	but
μέν . . . δέ	on the one hand . . . but
πλήν	but, nevertheless, however, yet

Purpose

ἵνα	in order that
μήποτε	lest, that . . . not (negative purpose)
ὅπως	in order that, that
ὥστε	for the purpose of

Result

ἵνα	in order that, so that
ὥστε	for the result that

Inference

ἄρα	consequently, therefore, then, thus, so
γάρ	for, thus
διό	therefore, for this reason
διότι	therefore
οὖν	therefore, thus, so
ὥστε	therefore, thus, so

Causal/Reason

γάρ	because, for, since

διότι	because, for
ἐπεί	because, since
ἐπειδή	because, since
καθώς	because
ὅτι	because, for
ὡς	because

Condition

εἰ	if, whether
ἐάν	if

Concession

εἰ καί	though, although

Modal Conjunctions (How)

Comparison

καθάπερ	as, just as
καθώς	as, just as
ὡς	as, like
ὡσεί	as, like
ὥσπερ	as, just as, like

Example

καί	that is, namely

Emphatic Conjunctions

γέ	indeed
δή	indeed
ναί	yes!, indeed

NOMINAL

We can use the label NOMINAL to refer to any word that does not function as a verb in a clause. A nominal may be

➤ a noun/substantive;

➤ a pronoun;

➤ an adjective;

➤ a participle;

➤ an infinitive (when not used as a verb);

➤ a preposition.

NOUN

A **NOUN** is a word that names something.

ENGLISH

Here are some classifications that nouns name:

➤ person	Jesus, Paul, Mary, father, sister
➤ place	town, country, Israel, Rome, Antioch
➤ animal	donkey, fish, dove
➤ thing	house, gate, road, Sabbath
➤ activity	running, birth, death
➤ idea or concept	truth, peace, righteousness
➤ quality	beauty

A **COMMON NOUN** is one that does *not* state the name of a specific person, place, etc. In English, a common noun begins with a lower case letter, unless, of course, it starts a sentence. In the list above, all nouns that are lower case are common nouns. Some use the label **SUBSTANTIVE** for this type of word.

A **PROPER NOUN** is one that *does* state the name of a specific person, etc. In English, this type of noun is capitalized. In the list above, all nouns with capital letters are proper nouns.

A **COMPOUND NOUN** is made up of more than one word: *ice cream, Jordan Rift*.

BIBLICAL GREEK

Nouns generally have the same function in Biblical Greek as they do in English. We need to keep track of certain items associated with nouns in Biblical Greek.

➤ gender (see **GENDER**, p. 30)

➤ number (see **NUMBER**, p. 32)

➤ function: a noun can have a range of functions in clauses (see the chapter CLAUSE, p. 193). Declension is one means of knowing a noun's function.

PRONOUN

A **PRONOUN** is a classification of words we can use as a substitute for a noun (see NOUN, p. 119) or noun phrase. It can refer therefore to a person, place, animal, thing, activity, idea or concept, etc.

We repeat the proper noun *Paul* in the following two sentences:

> Paul left Antioch.
>
> Paul went to Cyprus.

We can, instead, replace the second occurrence of *Paul* with a pronoun:

> Paul left Antioch.
>
> *He* went to Cyprus.

Commonly we use a pronoun after we have first mentioned the noun to which the pronoun refers. In such a case, the noun that the pronoun replaces is known as the **ANTECEDENT**. This use of the pronoun is known as **ANAPHORA** or **ANAPHORIC** use because it *brings back* the noun, so to speak (Greek ἀναφέρειν *to bring back*).

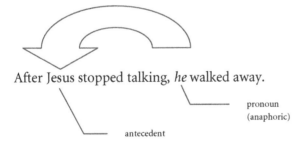

After Jesus stopped talking, *he* walked away.

                                               pronoun
                                               (anaphoric)

                         antecedent

Sometimes we use a pronoun *before* we have mentioned the noun to which the pronoun refers. In that case, the noun that the pronoun replaces is known as the **POSTCEDENT**. This use of the pronoun is known as **CATAPHORA** or **CATAPHORIC** use or, more commonly, **PROLEPSIS** or **PROLEPTIC** use. The pronoun refers to what follows.

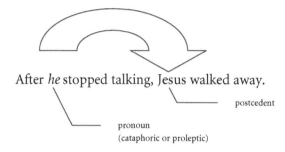

After *he* stopped talking, Jesus walked away.

postcedent

pronoun
(cataphoric or proleptic)

The noun to which a pronoun refers, *regardless* of whether it is the antecedent or the postcedent, can also be called the REFERENT. I prefer this term in the discussions ahead.

ENGLISH

We have several types of pronouns in English, the most important of which follow.

PERSONAL PRONOUN

These pronouns refer to different persons or entities. They change their form depending on their function in a clause.

➤ SUBJECT PERSONAL PRONOUN: Personal pronouns can be used as the subject of a verb (see SUBJECT, p. 198).

> *I* talked, and *you* listened.
>
>> *Who* talked? *I* = subject
>>
>> *I* is the subject of the verb *talked*
>>
>> *Who* listened? *You* = subject
>>
>> *You* is the subject of *listened*

	Singular	**Plural**
1st person	**I** (common) the person speaking	**we** (common) the person speaking + others
2d person	**you** (common) the person spoken to	**you** (common) the persons spoken to
3d person	**he** (masculine) **she** (feminine) **it** (neuter) the entity spoken about	**they** (common) the entities spoken about

Figure 18: English Subject Personal Pronouns

➢ **OBJECT PERSONAL PRONOUN**: Personal pronouns can be used as the object of a verb or the object of a preposition.

Herod saw *him* but spoke to *us.*

> Herod saw *whom? him* = object of verb
>
> *him* is the object of the verb *saw*

> Herod spoke *to whom? us* = object of preposition
>
> *us* is the object of the preposition *to*

	Singular	**Plural**
1st person	**me** (common) the person speaking	**us** (common) the person speaking + others
2d person	**you** (common) the person spoken to	**you** (common) the persons spoken to
3d person	**him** (masculine) **her** (feminine) **it** (neuter) the entity spoken about	**them** (common) the entities spoken about

Figure 19: English Object Personal Pronouns

POSSESSIVE PRONOUN

These pronouns replace a noun and specify the *possessor* of the replaced noun. The replacement of a noun is what distinguishes a possessive pronoun from a possessive adjective, which only modifies an existing noun (see POSSESSIVE ADJECTIVE, p. 161, under ADJECTIVE).

> Herodias and Herod had different desires. *Hers* was for revenge. *His* was to keep a promise.

As a comparison, look at the following similar sentences, which use possessive *adjectives:*

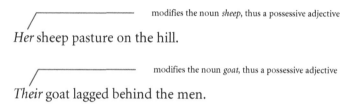

modifies the noun *sheep*, thus a possessive adjective

Her sheep pasture on the hill.

modifies the noun *goat*, thus a possessive adjective

Their goat lagged behind the men.

	Singular	Plural
1st person	**mine** (common) the person speaking	**ours** (common) the person speaking + others
2d person	**yours** (common) the person spoken to	**yours** (common) the persons spoken to
3d person	**his** (masculine) **hers** (feminine) **its** (neuter) the entity spoken about	**theirs** (common) the entities spoken about

Figure 20: English Possessive Personal Pronouns

INTERROGATIVE PRONOUN

Interrogative pronouns replace a noun and introduce a question. We use different pronouns on the basis of whether the replaced noun refers to something *animate* or something *inanimate*.

➢ ANIMATE

• **Who** takes the place of the subject of a verb.

> *Who* lives in the palace?
> └── subject

• **Whom** takes the place of the object of a verb or preposition (colloquially, American English speakers commonly use *who* rather than *whom,* the "prestige" form).[32]

> *Whom* did you see in the palace? [Colloquial: *Who* did you see in the
> └── object of verb   palace?]

> To *whom* did you give the letter? [Colloquial: *Who* did you give the let-
> └── object of preposition   ter to?]

• **Whose** is used in questions of possession or ownership.

> The disciples found the donkey. *Whose* is it?
> The disciples have his donkey. *Whose* do you have?

➢ INANIMATE: **What** takes the place of the subject or object of a verb or the object a preposition.

> *What* happened?
> └── subject

> *What* did you see in the palace?
> └── object of verb

> With *what* did you write the letter? [Colloquial: *What* did you write the letter
> └── object of preposition   with?]

---

[32] As I mentioned in the introduction, within the halls of the academy, the commonest surroundings I envision for this textbook, it is pedagogically useful to use English's acrolect, its *prestige* forms, while pointing out pertinent *colloquial* forms. The academy, on occasion, still expects the acrolect of its students.

INDEFINITE PRONOUN

These pronouns replace nouns and refer to entities without regard for whether they are known or identified. We can group many (but not all) of them into two primary bundles.

(1) Here follows the *one–body* bundle: *one* and *body* combine with other words.

someone	somebody
anyone	anybody
everyone	everybody
no one (none)	nobody

(2) The *many–few* (plus their relatives) bundle includes the following pronouns.

many	few
all	each
some	any
both	one
others	other/another
several	

Some indefinite *pronouns* function as *adjectives.* Do not confuse them. The former *replaces* a noun whereas the latter *modifies* a noun, usually by standing before the noun. Here are examples of the indefinite *pronoun:*

Someone whispered to the Pharisees.

Many saw the miracles.

The *other* lagged behind.

He healed a *few.*

As a comparison, look at the following similar sentences, which use *adjectives:*

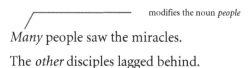
modifies the noun *people*

Many people saw the miracles.

The *other* disciples lagged behind.

DEMONSTRATIVE PRONOUN

These pronouns replace nouns; we categorize these pronouns according to whether they are NEAR (at hand) or REMOTE (farther/further away),[33] and SINGULAR or PLURAL. English makes no distinction for gender. Do not confuse a demonstrative *pronoun* with a demonstrative *adjective* (see DEMONSTRATIVE ADJECTIVE, p. 163). The former *replaces* a noun whereas the latter *modifies* a noun, usually by standing before the noun.

refers to the ram at hand (near)

This is the ram.

These are the sheep on the hill.

That is the goat that lagged behind.

The stubborn ones are *those.*

refers to stubborn ones farther away

As a comparison, look at the following similar sentences, which use demonstrative *adjectives:*

modifies the noun *ram*, which is at hand (near)

This ram belongs to him.

These sheep pasture on the hill.

That goat lagged behind *those* men.

Those mules are stubborn.

	Near	Remote
Singular	this	that
Plural	these	those

Figure 21: English Demonstrative Pronouns

---

[33] In English, we say "farther away" when *space* is in view, and "further away" when *time* and other *nonspatial* relationships are in view.

REFLEXIVE PRONOUN

Reflexive pronouns refer back to the subject of a clause. Commonly they *reflect* the verb's process in some way back to the subject. In sentence structure/syntax, they are often objects of a verb or of a preposition. Semantically, they frequently have the role of BENEFICIARY (for a definition, see SEMANTIC ROLES, p. 206, in the chapter SEMANTICS: PROCESSES, ROLES, AND CIRCUMSTANCES).

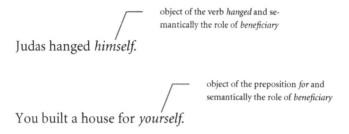

object of the verb *hanged* and semantically the role of *beneficiary*

Judas hanged *himself.*

object of the preposition *for* and semantically the role of *beneficiary*

You built a house for *yourself.*

	Singular	Plural
1st person	**myself** (common) the person speaking	**ourselves** (common) the person speaking + others
2d person	**yourself** (common) the person spoken to	**yourselves** (common) the persons spoken to
3d person	**himself** (masculine) **herself** (feminine) **itself** (neuter) the entity spoken about	**themselves** (common) the entities spoken about

Figure 22: English Reflexive Pronouns

RECIPROCAL PRONOUN

These pronouns indicate that two or more entities are interacting with each other. They are *reciprocating.* If two entities are in mind, the interaction goes in both directions. If more than two are in mind, the interaction can be in various combinations.

128

In English, the reciprocal pronoun tends to be a **PHRASE** (two or more words without predication): *one another* or *each other* are the most common.

The disciples fed *one another.*

They built houses for *each other.*

RELATIVE PRONOUN

These pronouns serve two primary functions:

1. They represent a previously mentioned noun or pronoun, which is known as the **REFERENT**, or **ANTECEDENT**, or **HEAD**. (Each of the labels is truly inter-changeable. We shall settle on the first label for the following discussion.)

   Jesus spoke to the woman *who* stood at the well.

   referent

2. They introduce a **RELATIVE CLAUSE** (though a preposition governing the rela-tive pronoun may come before the relative pronoun). A relative clause is a type of dependent/subordinate clause. That is, it is a clause that does not stand on its own and must be linked to a previous clause, which may be a main clause or another dependent/subordinate clause (see **CLAUSE**, p. 193). A relative clause may be either **RESTRICTIVE** or **NONRESTRICTIVE**, the discussion of which we shall explore later in this subsection.

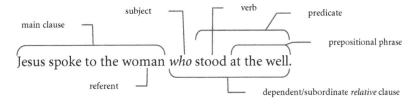

> *Who stood at the well* is not a free-standing clause. In this particular sentence *who* is a relative pronoun introducing the relative clause.

The form of the relative pronoun depends on (1) its syntactic function within the relative clause and (2) whether the referent is animate or inani-mate. A relative pronoun may function within the relative clause as

- a subject;

- an object of a verb or preposition;

- a possessive.

➢ **SUBJECT** OF A RELATIVE CLAUSE

We use different relative pronouns depending on whether the referent is animate or inanimate.

- animate referent ➪ *who*

Jesus spoke to the woman *who* stood at the well.

Who is the subject of the verb *stood.*

- inanimate referent ➪ *which* or *that*

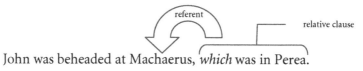

John was beheaded at Machaerus, *which* was in Perea.

Which is the subject of the verb *was.*

John was beheaded at a fortress *that* was in Perea.

That is the subject of the verb *was.*

➢ **OBJECT OF A VERB OR PREPOSITION** WITHIN A RELATIVE CLAUSE

We use different relative pronoun depending on whether the referent is animate or inanimate. English speakers commonly omit relative pronouns when they function as objects of verbs or prepositions within relative clauses. Here they are within parentheses as appropriate.

- animate referent ⇨ **whom**

A Samaritan was the woman (*whom*) Jesus saw.

Whom is the object of the verb *saw*; *Jesus* is the subject.

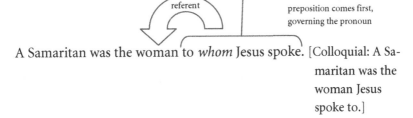

A Samaritan was the woman to *whom* Jesus spoke. [Colloquial: A Samaritan was the woman Jesus spoke to.]

Whom is the object of the preposition *to*.

- inanimate referent ⇨ **which** or **that**

John was beheaded at Machaerus, *which* Herod fortified.

Which is the object of the verb *fortified*; *Herod* is the subject.

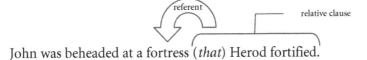

John was beheaded at a fortress (*that*) Herod fortified.

That is the object of the verb *fortified*; *Herod* is the subject.

131

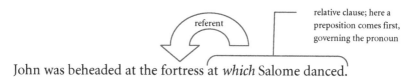

John was beheaded at the fortress at *which* Salome danced.

[Colloquial: John was beheaded at the fortress (*that*) Salome danced at.]

Which is the object of the preposition *at.*

➤ **POSSESSIVE** WITHIN A RELATIVE CLAUSE

The possessive modifier ***whose*** is a relative pronoun. Its form does not change regardless of its function or referent.

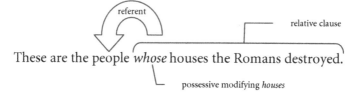

These are the people *whose* houses the Romans destroyed.

➤ **RESTRICTIVE** VERSUS **NONRESTRICTIVE** RELATIVE CLAUSES

A **RESTRICTIVE** relative clause *restricts* or *limits* the referent. Such a clause is essential to helping the reader or hearer understand the identity of the referent. In English these clauses do *not* use commas to set them off from the rest of the sentence. They are introduced by *who, whom, which,* or *that.*

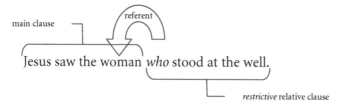

Jesus saw the woman *who* stood at the well.

The relative clause here is essential in identifying the referent, *the woman.* Envision a situation in which there might be many women. This relative clause restricts the referent to one particular woman whom Jesus saw at the well.

A **NONRESTRICTIVE** relative clause does *not* restrict or limit the referent. The referent is already clearly known. Such clauses simply offer more known information about a referent. In English these clauses do use commas to set them off from the rest of the sentence. They are introduced by *who, whom, which,* or *that.*

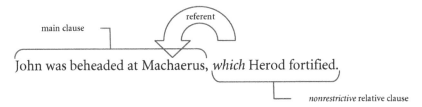

The relative clause here is not essential in identifying the referent, *Machaerus*. The clause is merely giving more known information about *Machaerus*. The clause is nonrestrictive.

BIBLICAL GREEK

PERSONAL PRONOUN

These pronouns refer to different persons or entities. They change their form depending on their function in a clause. For Biblical Greek, we should restructure how best to understand the personal pronoun. Particularly, we need to pay attention to case (see **CASE**, p. 34). Although we may talk of subject and object personal pronouns in English, we best talk of personal pronouns according to nominative case, accusative case, etc., in Biblical Greek.

➤ **NOMINATIVE-CASE PERSONAL PRONOUN**: These pronouns may stand in place of a noun in the nominative case. Beyond that, they often point out or highlight prominent information, whether it is, for example, contrast, clarity, or the subject of the clause (see **SUBJECT**, p. 198).

This nominative-case personal pronoun likely highlights both contrast and the subject of the clause. John answers the question "Who are you?" with this response. John is making the contrast that he is *not* Elijah (v. 21), and the pronoun is the subject of the clause.

ἐγὼ	φωνὴ	βοῶντος	ἐν	τῇ	ἐρήμῳ
I	voice	crying-out	in	the	wilderness

I am a voice crying out in the wilderness.

John 1:23

Here are the forms of the nominative-case personal pronouns:

	Singular	Plural
1st person	ἐγώ (common) the person speaking	ἡμεῖς (common) the person speaking + others
2d person	σύ (common the person spoken to	ὑμεῖς (common) the persons spoken to
3d person	αὐτός (masculine) αὐτή (feminine) αὐτό (neuter) the entity spoken about	αὐτοί (masculine) αὐταί (feminine) αὐτά (neuter) the entities spoken about

Figure 23: Biblical Greek Nominative-Case Personal Pronouns

➢ **ACCUSATIVE-CASE PERSONAL PRONOUN:** These personal pronouns commonly stand in place of a noun in the accusative case. They are, then, frequently pronouns that function as the object of a verb. Some prepositions take the accusative case. Where this occurs, the accusative personal pronoun is the object of a preposition.

• Object of a verb

καὶ	μὴ	εἰσενέγκῃς	**ἡμᾶς**	εἰς	πειρασμόν
and	not	you-lead	**us**	into	temptation

And do not lead *us* into temptation.

Matthew 6:13

- Object of a preposition

τότε	ἐξεπορεύετο	πρὸς	**αὐτὸν**	Ἱεροσόλυμα	Then Jerusalem went
then	it-goes-out	to	**him**	Jerusalem	out to *him.*

Matthew 3:5

Here are the forms of the accusative-case personal pronouns:

	Singular	**Plural**
1st person	ἐμέ, με (common)	ἡμᾶς (common)
	the person speaking	the person speaking + others
2d person	σέ, σε (common)	ὑμᾶς (common)
	the person spoken to	the persons spoken to
3d person	αὐτόν (masculine)	αὐτούς (masculine)
	αὐτήν (feminine)	αὐτάς (feminine)
	αὐτό (neuter)	αὐτά (neuter)
	the entity spoken about	the entities spoken about

Figure 24: Biblical Greek Accusative-Case Personal Pronouns

➤ **GENITIVE-CASE PERSONAL PRONOUN:** These personal pronouns usually convey *possession.* Biblical Greek does not possess a distinct possessive pronoun as English does (see p. 124). Rather, Biblical Greek takes a personal pronoun and casts it into the genitive case. This is one way—and a common way!—Biblical Greek conveys possession.

Here Biblical Greek and English have conceptual differences in how they routinely convey possession. English commonly conveys possession through a possessive *adjective: my* book, *your* book, *his* book, *her* book, etc. (see the subsection **POSSESSIVE ADJECTIVE** [p. 161] under **ENGLISH** in the chapter on **ADJECTIVE**). Biblical Greek, as mentioned, usually takes a personal pronoun and casts it into the genitive case.

Some prepositions take the genitive case (and can have little or nothing to do with possession). Where this occurs, the genitive personal pronoun is the object of the preposition.

- Genitive personal pronoun for possession

  ἡ μήτηρ **μου** καὶ οἱ ἀδελφοί **μου**   *my* mother and *my* brothers

  the mother **of-me** and the brothers **of-me**   Mark 3:34

- Object of a preposition

  μεθ' **ἡμῶν** ὁ   θεός   God (is) with *us.*

  with **us**   the God   Matthew 1:23

Here are the forms of the genitive-case personal pronouns:

	Singular	Plural
1st person	**ἐμοῦ, μου** (common)	**ἡμῶν** (common)
	the person speaking	the person speaking + others
2d person	**σοῦ, σου** (common)	**ὑμῶν** (common)
	the person spoken to	the persons spoken to
3d person	**αὐτοῦ** (masculine)	**αὐτῶν** (masculine)
	αὐτῆς (feminine)	**αὐτῶν** (feminine)
	αὐτοῦ (neuter)	**αὐτῶν** (neuter)
	the entity spoken about	the entities spoken about

Figure 25: Biblical Greek Genitive-Case Personal Pronouns

➢ **DATIVE-CASE PERSONAL PRONOUN:** These personal pronouns commonly stand in place of a noun in the dative case. Some prepositions take the dative case. Where this occurs, the dative personal pronoun is the object of a preposition.

καὶ λέγει **αὐτοῖς** ὁ   Ἰησοῦς   Jesus said to *them.*

and he-said **to-them** (the) Jesus   Matthew 15:34

136

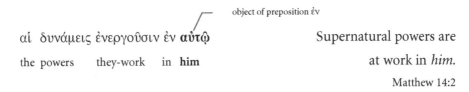

object of preposition ἐν

αἱ δυνάμεις ἐνεργοῦσιν ἐν **αὐτῷ**

the powers   they-work   in **him**

Supernatural powers are

at work in *him.*

Matthew 14:2

Here are the forms of the dative-case personal pronouns:

	Singular	**Plural**
1st person	**ἐμοί, μοι** (common) the person speaking	**ἡμῖν** (common) the person speaking + others
2d person	**σοί, σοι** (common) the person spoken to	**ὑμῖν** (common) the persons spoken to
3d person	**αὐτῷ** (masculine) **αὐτῇ** (feminine) **αὐτῷ** (neuter) the entity spoken about	**αὐτοῖς** (masculine) **αὐταῖς** (feminine) **αὐτοῖς** (neuter) the entities spoken about

Figure 26: Biblical Greek Dative-Case Personal Pronouns

A SPECIAL PRONOUN: THE SO-CALLED "INTENSIVE" PRONOUN, αὐτός

Here we add a category not covered in our treatment of English pronouns. We need to discuss the Biblical Greek word αὐτός.

You likely have just read the portion above on personal pronouns, where you saw that αὐτός functioned as a 3d-person personal pronoun. From the perspective of the history of the Greek language, αὐτός was *not* a 3d-person personal pronoun. It took on this role, however. Homer used a 3d-person personal pronoun that was not αὐτός. From the Attic dialect of Greek, we catch glimpses of a "true" third person pronoun, used in limited fashion: οἷ (3d, singular, dative) and σφίσι(ν) (3d, plural, dative). Even in Attic, though, these attested pronouns were functioning as reflexives, and αὐτός was already beginning to be used as a 3d-person personal pronoun—a role it certainly plays within Biblical Greek.[34]

Many Greek grammars call αὐτός an INTENSIVE pronoun. Be aware of this, but get into the habit of calling it according to its role when you encounter it in text. Here are three of its common functions: (1) a PERSONAL PRONOUN, (2) an IDENTIFYING ADJECTIVE, and (3) a FOCUS PRONOUN.

➤ PERSONAL PRONOUN: We have already treated this function in the previous section on PERSONAL PRONOUN (see p. 133–137). αὐτός may function as a 3d-person personal pronoun.

➤ IDENTIFYING ADJECTIVE: αὐτός may be an adjective, used *attributively,* to identify a noun, usually in the sense of "same" (for example, "the *same* hour").

The format, or syntax, in which we generally find this function of αὐτός is *article + adjective + noun.* This is one of several formats or syntaxes in Biblical Greek for adjectival *attribution.* That is, the adjective offers an *attribute* about the noun; it *modifies* the noun. (For more on this concept, read DESCRIPTIVE ADJECTIVE for English and Biblical Greek, pp. 158, 164.)

article + adjective + noun

ἄλλῳ   δὲ   λόγος   γνώσεως   κατὰ   τὸ   **αὐτὸ**   πνεῦμα
to-another but word   of-knowledge according-to the **same** spirit

but to another, a word of knowledge according to the *same* spirit
1 Corinthians 12:8

➤ FOCUS PRONOUN: By *focus* we refer to a linguistic term that attaches importance or salience usually to a word or phrase. A word or phrase that is in focus is one that is prominent or most salient. It is in focus, so to speak.

---

[34] Herbert Weir Smyth, *Greek Grammar* (rev. Gordon M. Messing; Cambridge: Harvard University Press, 1956), 90–92.

Clear examples of this function are in a format or syntax where αὐτός occurs *not in an attributive position* like the identifying adjective function but *in the same clause with, in the same syntactic position as* (usually the subject), and *in addition to* an explicitly stated entity to which αὐτός refers. The stated referent of αὐτός may be a noun, a proper name, or the subject of a verbal form that, simply by the verb's form, already refers to or encodes the subject.

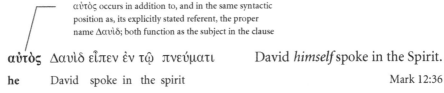

αὐτὴ occurs in addition to, and in the same syntactic position as, its explicitly stated referent, the articular noun ἡ κτίσις; both function as the subject in the clause

αὐτὴ	ἡ	κτίσις	ἐλευθερωθήσεται	ἀπὸ	τῆς	δουλείας
she		the creation	she-will-be-set-free	from	the	slavery

Creation *herself* will be set free from slavery. Romans 8:21

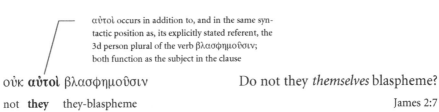

αὐτὸς occurs in addition to, and in the same syntactic position as, its explicitly stated referent, the proper name Δαυίδ; both function as the subject in the clause

αὐτὸς	Δαυὶδ	εἶπεν	ἐν	τῷ	πνεύματι
he	David	spoke	in	the	spirit

David *himself* spoke in the Spirit. Mark 12:36

αὐτοὶ occurs in addition to, and in the same syntactic position as, its explicitly stated referent, the 3d person plural of the verb βλασφημοῦσιν; both function as the subject in the clause

οὐκ	αὐτοὶ	βλασφημοῦσιν
not	they	they-blaspheme

Do not they *themselves* blaspheme? James 2:7

The main point is that Biblical Greek is making something in a clause prominent; it is bringing it into focus. A helpful way to convey that prominence or focus can be through using *himself, herself, itself, themselves,* etc., in your translation, as I have done with the examples above. But do not let that confuse you about pronouns. To convey what is focused in the Biblical Greek text, I have used English reflexive pronouns (see p. 127). The Greek, of course, is *not* using a reflexive pronoun (see p. 150). It is using αὐτός as a focus pronoun.

139

POSSESSIVE PRONOUN

What generally functions as a possessive adjective (ἐμός, σός, etc.) may function, in a few instances, as a possessive pronoun in Biblical Greek. In those few places, the possessive is not an adjective modifying a noun but standing in place of a noun. You may consult figure 37 on p. 173 for the forms of the possessive. That table is for possessive adjectives, but the form is identical for when they function as pronouns.

More commonly, Biblical Greek conveys possession by (1) casting the personal pronoun into the genitive case and (2) using possessive adjectives such as ἐμός, σός, etc. (See the discussion under **POSSESSIVE ADJECTIVE**, pp. 161, 172.)

ὑμετέρα	ἐστὶν	ἡ	βασιλεία	τοῦ	θεοῦ	*Yours* is the Kingdom of God.
yours	she-is	the	kingdom	of-the	God	Luke 6:20

INTERROGATIVE PRONOUN

Interrogative pronouns replace a nominal and introduce a question. Biblical Greek's inventory of this kind of pronoun leads us to see that it includes three major types. (1) One type asks for or seeks out IDENTITY, that is, "who?" or "what?" (2) Another asks for QUALITY, "what sort?" or "what kind?" (3) The third asks for QUANTITY, "how many?" or "how much?"

Interrogative pronouns, as Biblical Greek grammars label them, do *not,* however, always function as pronouns. These "pronouns" sometimes function as adjectives. This is not uncommon among pronouns. Demonstratives can function as pronouns and as adjectives, and I treat them separately in this book according to their function. The Biblical Greek indefinite pronoun can function as a pronoun or as an adjective.

We need to understand, then, that the label *interrogative pronoun* is simply a label within the discipline of Biblical Greek. The label does not always correctly describe the interrogative's precise function in a text. When an interrogative pronoun is truly a pronoun, then the label fits. When an interrogative "pronoun" functions as an adjective, we ought to understand it as an "interrogative adjective."

This section treats *only* the interrogative pronoun when it functions as a *pronoun*. A "true" interrogative pronoun is one that stands in place of a nominal; that is, it replaces it: *"Who* saw Jesus?" or *"What* is Peter doing in Capernaum?" (An interrogative adjective *modifies* a nominal, it does not *replace* it.)

For an interrogative when it functions as an adjective, see INTERROGATIVE ADJECTIVE, pp. 162, 174, under ADJECTIVE.

Interrogative Pronoun for IDENTITY

Biblical Greek does not use different pronouns based *solely* on whether the referent is something animate or inanimate. Often, though, τίς, the form that refers to masculine and feminine grammatical entities, will refer to animate things when grammatical gender coincides with the biological gender of something animate. Thus τίς often is translated as "who?"

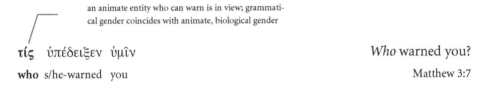

an animate entity who can warn is in view; grammatical gender coincides with animate, biological gender

τίς ὑπέδειξεν ὑμῖν *Who* warned you?

who s/he-warned you Matthew 3:7

τίς will, however, have to be translated "what?" or "which?" when, while referring to a masculine or feminine grammatical entity, it refers to a word that to an English speaker is inanimate.

τίς best conveyed in English as "what/which" because referents χρυσός and ναός, to an English speaker, are inanimate

τίς γὰρ μείζων ἐστίν ὁ χρυσὸς ἢ ὁ ναὸς

what for more-important it-is the gold or the temple

What/which is more important, the gold or the temple . . . ? Matthew 23:17

τί, the form that refers to neuter grammatical gender, is often conveyed in English as "what?"

τί λέγει ἡ γραφή   *What* does Scripture say?

what says-she the Scripture   Galatians 4:30

τί is sometimes best understood as equivalent to English "why?" although this does not strike an English speaker as asking for identity. Usually τί is in the accusative case when this occurs. We probably ought to understand τί functioning as an *adverbial adjunct accusative of specification* (see **ADVERBIAL ADJUNCT**, p. 48, and **ANATOMY OF A VERBAL CLAUSE**, p. 195). It is asking to specify something. For example, *"Of what (τί) specifically* are you afraid?" or *"As to what (τί) specifically* are you afraid?" is commonly conveyed in English by using "why": *"Why* are you afraid?"

τί used in accusative case likely as adverbial accusative of specification

τί   δειλοί ἐστε   *Why* are you afraid?

as-to-what afraid   are-you   Mark 4:40

Biblical Greek interrogative pronouns can take the place of a subject of a verb, an object of a verb or preposition (like English), and other relationships appropriate to the case into which it is cast.

τίς as subject of the clause

τίς ὑπέδειξεν ὑμῖν   *Who* warned you?

who s/he-warned you   Matthew 3:7

τίς as object of the clause

τίνα ζητεῖτε   *Whom* do you seek?

whom you-seek   John 18:4

Whereas English uses "whose" for questions of possession and ownership, Biblical Greek commonly uses τίς/τί in the genitive case, the same case that, when applied to personal pronouns, commonly conveys possession.

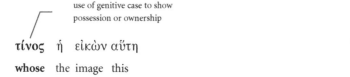

use of genitive case to show possession or ownership

τίνος ἡ εἰκὼν αὕτη   *Whose* image is this?

whose the image this   Matthew 22:20

Here are the forms of τίς/τί:

		masculine/ feminine	neuter
Singular	nom	τίς	τί
	acc	τίνα	τί
	gen	τίνος	τίνος
	dat	τίνι	τίνι
Plural	nom	τίνες	τίνα
	acc	τίνας	τίνα
	gen	τίνων	τίνων
	dat	τίσι(ν)	τίσι(ν)

Figure 27: Biblical Greek Identifying Interrogative Pronouns

Interrogative Pronoun for QUALITY

One interrogative pronoun asks "what sort?" or "what kind?" It is ποῖος.

καὶ εἶπεν αὐτοῖς, **ποῖα**	He said to them,
and he-said to-them, **What-kind-of-things**	*"What kind of things?"*
	Luke 24:19

Interrogative Pronoun for QUANTITY

One interrogative pronoun asks "how many?" or "how much?" It is πόσος.

οὐκ ἀκούεις **πόσα** σου καταμαρτυροῦσιν	Don't you hear
not hear-you **how-many-things** you they-testify-against	*how many things* they
	testify against you?
	Matthew 27:13

INDEFINITE PRONOUN

These pronouns replace a nominal and refer to entities without regard for whether they are known or identified. In Biblical Greek we account for NUMBER (singular and plural), GENDER, and CASE. The indefinite pronoun's form is identical to the interrogative's, apart from the accents. Do not confuse an indefinite *pronoun* with an indefinite *adjective* (see **INDEFINITE ADJECTIVE**, p. 175). The former *replaces* a noun whereas the latter *modifies* a noun.

εἴδομέν **τινα** ...	ἐκβάλλοντα δαιμόνια	We saw *someone* ...
we-saw **someone** ... casting-out demons		casting out demons.
		Luke 9:49

Here are the forms of τις/τι:

		masculine/ feminine	neuter
Singular	nom	τις	τι
	acc	τινά	τι
	gen	τινός	τινός
	dat	τινί	τινί
Plural	nom	τινές	τινά
	acc	τινάς	τινά
	gen	τινῶν	τινῶν
	dat	τισί(ν)	τισί(ν)

Figure 28: Biblical Greek Indefinite Pronouns

DEMONSTRATIVE PRONOUN

Biblical Greek, like English, has two *primary* demonstrative pronouns, one for the **NEAR** (at hand), οὗτος, and one for the **REMOTE** (farther/further away),[35] ἐκεῖνος. In Biblical Greek we account for **NUMBER** (singular and plural), **GENDER**, and **CASE**. Again, do not confuse a demonstrative *pronoun* with a demonstrative *adjective* (see **DEMONSTRATIVE ADJECTIVE**, p. 176). The former *replaces* a noun whereas the latter *modifies* a noun.

---

[35] In English, we say "farther away" when *space* is in view and "further away" when *time* and other *nonspatial* relationships are in view.

In addition to the near demonstrative οὗτος, Biblical Greek also uses ὅδε, though only in ten instances. In Classical Greek οὗτος was anaphoric, referring solely back to the antecedent; ὅδε was cataphoric, referring solely forward to the post-cedent (see p. 121 for definitions). That distinction does not hold true in Biblical Greek.

οὗτός ἐστιν ὁ υἱός μου ὁ ἀγαπητός		*This* is my beloved son.
this he-is the son of-me the beloved		Matthew 3:17

ἐκεῖνος ἦν ὁ λύχνος		*That one* was the lamp.
that he-was the lamp		John 5:35

Here are the forms of οὗτος:

		masculine	feminine	neuter
Singular	nom	οὗτος	αὕτη	τοῦτο
	acc	τοῦτον	ταύτην	τοῦτο
	gen	τούτου	ταύτης	τούτου
	dat	τούτῳ	ταύτῃ	τούτῳ
Plural	nom	οὗτοι	αὗται	ταῦτα
	acc	τούτους	ταύτας	ταῦτα
	gen	τούτων	τούτων	τούτων
	dat	τούτοις	ταύταις	τούτοις

Figure 29: Biblical Greek Near Demonstrative Pronouns

Here are the forms of ἐκεῖνος:

		masculine	feminine	neuter
Singular	nom	ἐκεῖνος	ἐκείνη	ἐκεῖνο
	acc	ἐκεῖνον	ἐκείνην	ἐκεῖνο
	gen	ἐκείνου	ἐκείνης	ἐκείνου
	dat	ἐκείνῳ	ἐκείνῃ	ἐκείνῳ
Plural	nom	ἐκεῖνοι	ἐκεῖναι	ἐκεῖνα
	acc	ἐκείνους	ἐκείνας	ἐκεῖνα
	gen	ἐκείνων	ἐκείνων	ἐκείνων
	dat	ἐκείνοις	ἐκείναις	ἐκείνοις

Figure 30: Biblical Greek Remote Demonstrative Pronouns

A number of Biblical Greek grammars discuss the demonstrative in ways that, through the eyes of a first-year student, are a challenge. At the very least, the discussions come across as a hurdle of confusing terminology; at the very most, the discussions might be less than accurate. The excursus that follows addresses this topic.

Excursus: On the Structure/Syntax of Demonstratives

One of the quirks of some Greek-teaching grammars is labeling a word a "pronoun" when it actually functions as an *adjective*.[36] Do not to confuse the two. I first addressed the issue above under INTERROGATIVE PRONOUN, p. 140.

Another quirk, certainly in the eyes of students, is when grammars routinely describe the demonstrative functioning as an adjective in a "predicate" adjective position, despite the demonstrative *not* being an adjective used predicatively. The

---

[36] For example, from Black's grammar: "[Demonstratives] are most frequently used to modify nouns . . . the *demonstrative pronoun* [emphasis added] stands in the predicate position" (Black, *Learn to Read New Testament Greek,* 74). If a demonstrative is used to modify a noun, it is best to call it an adjective, yet one reads that it is still being labeled a demonstrative *pronoun.*

grammars nevertheless translate their examples as *attributive* adjectives,[37] though they called them *predicate* ones. (See the discussion DESCRIPTIVE ADJECTIVE under ADJECTIVE, pp. 158, 164, for a clarification of attributive and predicate adjectives in English and Biblical Greek.) For example,

οὗτος ὁ λόγος   would be translated   *This* word.

this   the word

Let us explore the confusion, replacing οὗτος with a bona fide adjective, ἀγαθός. Students learn that a predicate adjective is one that is the predicate of a clause; that is, it makes a comment about a grammatical subject. They learn that the structure or syntax of predicate adjectives is the following:

ἀγαθὸς ὁ   λόγος   *Good* is the word.

good   the word

ὁ   λόγος **ἀγαθός**   The word is *good*.

the word   good

The adjective in both these cases is described as being in the predicate position. It is making a comment about the grammatical subject, here ὁ λόγος. Students are confused, then, by grammars that talk of demonstratives being in a predicate position but translate them in an *attributive* position. Here are some biblical examples taken from Black's grammar:[38]

οὗτοι οἱ λόγοι πιστοὶ καὶ ἀληθινοί   *These* words are faithful and true.

these the words faithful and true   Revelation 22:6

ἔλεγεν   δὲ **ταύτην** τὴν παραβολήν   He was speaking *this* parable.

he-speaks then **this**   the parable   Luke 13:6

---

[37]For example, William D. Mounce, *Basics of Biblical Greek: Grammar* (Grand Rapids, Mich.: Zondervan, 1993), 104; Black, *Learn to Read New Testament Greek,* 75.

[38] Black, *Learn to Read New Testament Greek,* 75.

ἀγοράζει τὸν ἀγρὸν **ἐκεῖνον**   He buys *that* field.

he-buys   the field   that   Matthew 13:44

In the first example, if in the clause we read nothing more than οὗτοι οἱ λόγοι, we would understand that we have true predication separating οὗτοι and οἱ λόγοι, *These are the words.* But the clause has other words, and in the end, we have to see a structure/syntax where the words οὗτοι οἱ λόγοι constitute the grammatical subject while πιστοὶ καὶ ἀληθινοί comprise the predicate.

There lies the confusion. The student reads that in such clauses the demonstrative *pronoun(!)* is in a *predicate(!)* position (a label borrowed from adjectival syntax). It is, however, not a predicate and is translated into English as an *attributive adjective!* What is going on?

One thing to understand is that Biblical Greek grammarians have simply found the phrase "predicate position" a convenient label to describe the word structure of

> demonstrative + arthrous noun (with article) or
>
> arthrous noun + demonstrative.

The demonstrative here, in *structure,* mimics predicate-adjective syntax. Referring to what he calls "pronominal adjectives" (words that function as pronouns and as adjectives, such as demonstratives and interrogatives), Wallace, in fact, says that they can "stand in a predicate *position* but have an attributive *relation* to the noun."[39] "Predicate position" seems to have become a convenient shorthand to refer to a particular word structure. Students, however, understandably can find this quite confusing.

But we might have more at stake here than just an arguably quirky label. With demonstratives in mind, we might consider another structural/syntactic phenomenon.

---

[39] Wallace, *The Basics of New Testament Syntax,* 308.

APPOSITION is a type of structure/syntax where (1) two or more individual words or phrases are juxtaposed (simply side by side), (2) refer to the same referent, and (3) sit within the same grammatical slot (subject, adverbial, etc.).

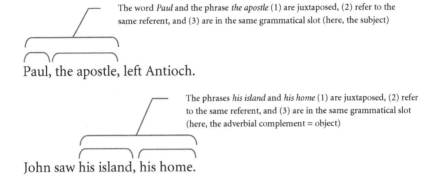

The word *Paul* and the phrase *the apostle* (1) are juxtaposed, (2) refer to the same referent, and (3) are in the same grammatical slot (here, the subject)

Paul, the apostle, left Antioch.

The phrases *his island* and *his home* (1) are juxtaposed, (2) refer to the same referent, and (3) are in the same grammatical slot (here, the adverbial complement = object)

John saw his island, his home.

Perhaps we can view a demonstrative + arthrous noun or arthrous noun + demonstrative structure/syntax as an instance of apposition—the apposition of a demonstrative *pronoun* and an arthrous noun. This might have the advantage of being a more straightforward and less cumbersome explanation. Our English translations, however, would remain as they are, using a structure/syntax very different from Biblical Greek. Whereas Biblical Greek is a syntax of apposition, English is a syntax of demonstrative attributive adjective. Let us revisit some earlier examples with this understanding.

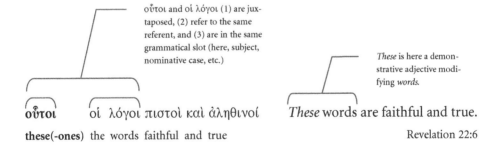

οὗτοι and οἱ λόγοι (1) are juxtaposed, (2) refer to the same referent, and (3) are in the same grammatical slot (here, subject, nominative case, etc.)

These is here a demonstrative adjective modifying *words*.

οὗτοι   οἱ λόγοι πιστοὶ καὶ ἀληθινοί

these(-ones) the words faithful and true

These words are faithful and true.

Revelation 22:6

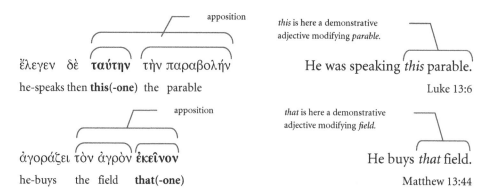

ἔλεγεν δὲ **ταύτην** τὴν παραβολήν

he-speaks then **this(-one)** the parable

this is here a demonstrative adjective modifying *parable.*

He was speaking *this* parable.

Luke 13:6

ἀγοράζει τὸν ἀγρὸν **ἐκεῖνον**

he-buys the field **that(-one)**

that is here a demonstrative adjective modifying *field.*

He buys *that* field.

Matthew 13:44

REFLEXIVE PRONOUN

Like English, Biblical Greek reflexive pronouns commonly *reflect* the process of the verb back to the subject. In sentence structure/syntax, they are often objects of a verb or of a preposition. Semantically, they frequently have the role of BENEFICIARY (for a definition, see SEMANTIC ROLES, p. 206 in the chapter SEMANTICS: PROCESSES, ROLES, AND CIRCUMSTANCES).

By virtue of their function in clauses, they *never* occur in the nominative case (because, in part, they are not the grammatical subject). Their form is a combination of the personal pronoun and the forms of the oblique cases (accusative, genitive, dative) of αὐτός. ἐμ– combines with the oblique cases of αὐτός to refer to the first person. σε– plus αὐτός refer to the second person, while ἑ– and αὐτός refer to the third person (ἑ– is a remnant from Homeric Greek, which used ἑέ/ἕ [accusative], εἷο/ἕο [genitive], and ἑοῖ/οἷ [dative] for the third person singular personal pronoun). Only one form, ἑ– plus the plural of αὐτός, inflected for case and gender but not person, is the plural reflexive pronoun.

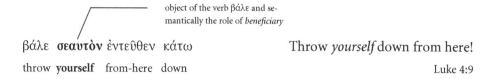

βάλε **σεαυτὸν** ἐντεῦθεν κάτω

throw **yourself** from-here down

object of the verb βάλε and semantically the role of *beneficiary*

Throw *yourself* down from here!

Luke 4:9

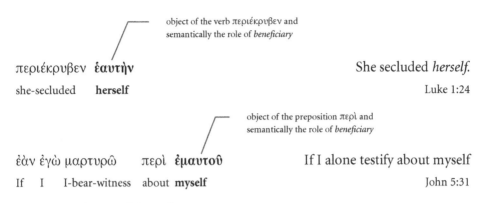

περιέκρυβεν **ἑαυτὴν**   She secluded *herself.*

she-secluded   **herself**   Luke 1:24

ἐὰν ἐγὼ μαρτυρῶ   περὶ **ἐμαυτοῦ**   If I alone testify about myself

If   I   I-bear-witness about **myself**   John 5:31

Here are the forms of the reflexive pronouns:

		Singular		Plural		
		masculine	feminine	masculine	feminine	neuter
1st person	acc	ἐμαυτόν	ἐμαυτήν	ἑαυτούς	ἑαυτάς	ἑαυτά
	gen	ἐμαυτοῦ	ἐμαυτῆς	ἑαυτῶν	ἑαυτῶν	ἑαυτῶν
	dat	ἐμαυτῷ	ἐμαυτῇ	ἑαυτοῖς	ἑαυταῖς	ἑαυτοῖς
		the person speaking		the person speaking + others		
2d person	acc	σεαυτόν	σεαυτήν	ἑαυτούς	ἑαυτάς	ἑαυτά
	gen	σεαυτοῦ	σεαυτῆς	ἑαυτῶν	ἑαυτῶν	ἑαυτῶν
	dat	σεαυτῷ	σεαυτῇ	ἑαυτοῖς	ἑαυταῖς	ἑαυτοῖς
		the person spoken to		the persons spoken to		
		masculine	feminine	neuter		
3d person	acc	ἑαυτόν	ἑαυτήν	ἑαυτό	ἑαυτούς	ἑαυτάς	ἑαυτά
	gen	ἑαυτοῦ	ἑαυτῆς	ἑαυτοῦ	ἑαυτῶν	ἑαυτῶν	ἑαυτῶν
	dat	ἑαυτῷ	ἑαυτῇ	ἑαυτῷ	ἑαυτοῖς	ἑαυταῖς	ἑαυτοῖς
		the entity spoken about			the entities spoken about		

Figure 31: Biblical Greek Reflexive Pronouns

RECIPROCAL PRONOUN

Like English, Biblical Greek reciprocal pronouns indicate that two or more entities are interacting with each other. They are *reciprocating.* If two entities are in
mind, the interaction goes in both directions. If more than two are in mind, the
interaction can be in various combinations. The forms of these pronouns have a
foundation, ἄλλος *another, other.* They never occur in the nominative case and
are always plural in number.

μὴ καταλαλεῖτε **ἀλλήλων**   Do not slander *one another!*

not slander **one-another**   James 4:11

ἐὰν ἀγάπην ἔχητε ἐν **ἀλλήλοις**   if you have love for *one another*

if love you-have for **one-another**   John 13:35

ἔβλεπον εἰς **ἀλλήλους** οἱ μαθηταὶ   The disciples looked at *one another.*

they-looked at **one-another** the disciples   John 13:22

Here are the forms of the reciprocal pronouns:

		Plural		
		masculine	feminine	neuter
All persons	acc	ἀλλήλους	–	–
	gen	ἀλλήλων	–	ἀλλήλων
	dat	ἀλλήλοις	–	ἀλλήλοις

Figure 32: Biblical Greek Reciprocal Pronouns

RELATIVE PRONOUN

Biblical Greek's relative pronouns are used for two types of relative clauses: (1)
the **DEPENDENT** or **ATTRIBUTIVE RELATIVE CLAUSE**, which modifies a referent, and
(2) the oddly labeled **INDEPENDENT RELATIVE CLAUSE**. The former is similar to
how English's relative pronoun functions—it is linked to a mentioned noun or

pronoun. The latter is independent and is not relative to another word or word group around it.

Classical Greek had what many grammars call a DEFINITE and INDEFINITE relative pronoun. Biblical Greek no longer has a fully productive indefinite relative pronoun used in all grammatical cases. We shall look in more detail at these later (p. 156).

The form of the relative pronoun in Biblical Greek, whether definite or indefinite, is tied to GENDER, NUMBER, and CASE. We shall revisit this as we look specifically at each of the two types of relative clauses.

Dependent or Attributive Relative Clause

As in English, the relative pronouns, when associated with dependent or attributive relative clauses, serve two primary functions.

1. They represent a mentioned noun/noun phrase or pronoun—the referent, antecedent, or head.

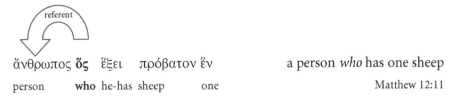

ἄνθρωπος ὃς ἕξει πρόβατον ἕν	a person *who* has one sheep
person **who** he-has sheep one	Matthew 12:11

2. They introduce a DEPENDENT or ATTRIBUTIVE RELATIVE CLAUSE (though a preposition that governs the pronoun may come first). This type of relative clause is a dependent/subordinate clause. That is, it is a clause that does not stand on its own and is linked to a previous clause, which may be a main clause or another dependent/subordinate clause (see CLAUSE, p. 193). The relative pronoun *usually* (but not always) agrees in GENDER and NUMBER with the referent. Expect the pronoun to agree, but do not be shocked if it does not. The CASE of the relative pronoun is *usually* linked to the role the pronoun plays within the relative clause. That is, the pronoun is tied to the structural or syntactic role it plays there. Exceptions, though, abound. Biblical Greek has no formal distinction between restrictive and nonrestrictive

relative clauses; no special punctuation or other written indicators convey the distinction that occurs in English.

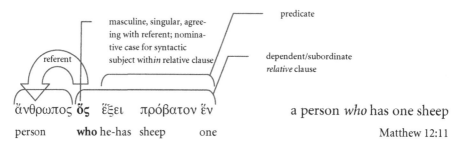

ὅς ἕξει πρόβατον ἕν is not a free-standing clause. In this particular sentence ὅς is a relative pronoun introducing a dependent/attributive relative clause within the sentence.

Although we may talk of a relative pronoun serving as a syntactic subject, an object of a verb or preposition, etc., we best talk of it according to its case within the dependent/attributive relative clause.

➤ **NOMINATIVE CASE** WITHIN A DEPENDENT/ATTRIBUTIVE RELATIVE CLAUSE

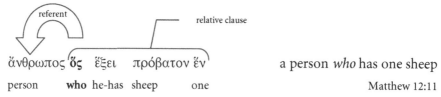

ὅς is masculine singular to match the referent; it is in the nominative case to serve as the syntactic subject of this verbal relative clause (see Verbal Predication, p. 201, under Predicate/Predication).

➢ **ACCUSATIVE CASE** WITHIN A DEPENDENT/ATTRIBUTIVE RELATIVE CLAUSE

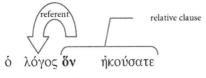

ὁ λόγος ὃν ἠκούσατε   the word *which* you heard

the word   **which** you-heard   1 John 2:7

ὅν is masculine singular to match the referent; it is in the accusative case to serve as the syntactic object of this verbal relative clause (see Verbal Predication, p. 201, under Predicate/Predication).

➢ **GENITIVE CASE** WITHIN A DEPENDENT/ATTRIBUTIVE RELATIVE CLAUSE

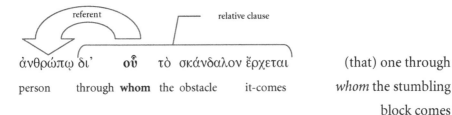

ἀνθρώπῳ δι’ οὗ τὸ σκάνδαλον ἔρχεται   (that) one through

person   through **whom** the obstacle   it-comes   *whom* the stumbling

block comes

Matthew 18:7

οὗ is masculine singular to match the referent; it is in the genitive case to serve as the syntactic object of a preposition, a prepositional phrase within the predicate.

➢ **DATIVE CASE** WITHIN A DEPENDENT/ATTRIBUTIVE RELATIVE CLAUSE

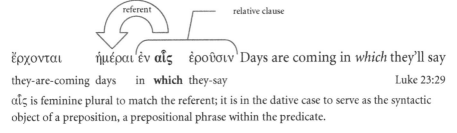

ἔρχονται   ἡμέραι ἐν αἷς ἐροῦσιν Days are coming in *which* they'll say

they-are-coming days   in **which** they-say   Luke 23:29

αἷς is feminine plural to match the referent; it is in the dative case to serve as the syntactic object of a preposition, a prepositional phrase within the predicate.

Independent Relative Clause

The oddly labeled independent relative clause is a clause that is not *relative* to another word or word-group around it. The whole clause, including the relative pronoun, can function as a basic syntactic element of (often) a main clause—as a subject (see **SUBJECT**, p. 198), for example, or as an adverbial (see under **VERBAL**

155

PREDICATION, p. 201, under **PREDICATE/PREDICATION**). The gender, number, and case of such a relative pronoun are tied to its referent and to its syntactic position in the (often a main) clause where the independent relative clause is found.

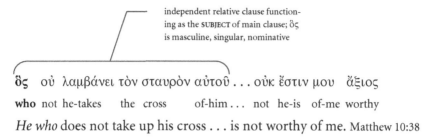

independent relative clause functioning as the SUBJECT of main clause; ὅς is masculine, singular, nominative

ὅς   οὐ λαμβάνει τὸν σταυρὸν αὐτοῦ . . . οὐκ ἔστιν μου   ἄξιος

who not he-takes   the cross   of-him . . . not he-is of-me worthy

He who does not take up his cross . . . is not worthy of me. Matthew 10:38

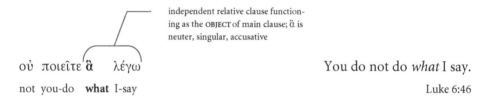

independent relative clause functioning as the OBJECT of main clause; ἃ is neuter, singular, accusative

οὐ ποιεῖτε ἃ   λέγω   You do not do *what* I say.

not you-do **what** I-say   Luke 6:46

Definite and Indefinite Relative Pronoun

Classical Greek had what grammarians usually call **DEFINITE** and **INDEFINITE** relative pronouns. The relative pronoun ὅς, by itself, was the definite, and the combination of the relative pronoun ὅς plus the indefinite pronoun τις produced ὅστις, the indefinite relative.

In Biblical Greek, the so-called indefinite relative pronoun can have in mind a **GENERIC** whole, "anyone who," "everyone who." Further, similar to a function of anarthrous (without an article) nouns (see pp. 109–112 in the **ARTICLE** chapter), the indefinite pronoun may focus on the **QUALITY** of a referent, that is, its essence, its nature.

"indefinite" relative pronoun most likely referring to a generic class, here of people

ὅστις   δ᾽ ἂν ἀρνήσηταί με   *whoever* denies me

whoever but   he-denies   me   Matthew 10:33

"indefinite" relative pronoun most likely referring to a generic class, here of people, whose nature is such that they exchange truth for a lie

οἵτινες μετήλλαξαν τὴν ἀλήθειαν τοῦ θεοῦ ἐν τῷ ψεύδει
who they-exchanged the truth of-the of-God for the lie

These ones (were of such a nature that they) exchanged God's truth for a lie. Romans 1:25

Here are the forms of the "definite" relative pronoun:

		masculine	feminine	neuter
Singular	nom	ὅς	ἥ	ὅ
	acc	ὅν	ἥν	ὅ
	gen	οὗ	ἧς	οὗ
	dat	ᾧ	ᾗ	ᾧ
Plural	nom	οἵ	αἵ	ἅ
	acc	οὕς	ἅς	ἅ
	gen	ὧν	ὧν	ὧν
	dat	οἷς	αἷς	οἷς

Figure 33: Biblical Greek "Definite" Relative Pronouns

Here are the forms of the "indefinite" relative pronoun:

		masculine	feminine	neuter
Singular	nom	ὅστις	ἥτις	ὅ τι
	acc	–	–	–
	gen	–	–	–
	dat	–	–	–
Plural	nom	οἵτινες	αἵτινες	ἅτινα
	acc	–	–	–
	gen	–	–	–
	dat	–	–	–

Figure 34: Biblical Greek "Indefinite" Relative Pronouns

ADJECTIVE

An **ADJECTIVE** is a word that modifies or describes a noun or a pronoun. We classify adjectives generally according to how they describe a noun or pronoun. They are **ADNOMINAL** phenomena; that is, they are most closely linked *to nouns,* precisely what *ad-nominal* means. As a contrast, adverbs are most closely linked to verbs, *ad-verb.*

ENGLISH

The main types of adjectives we see in English are (1) descriptive, (2) possessive, (3) interrogative, (4) indefinite, and (5) demonstrative.

DESCRIPTIVE ADJECTIVE

A descriptive adjective describes a characteristic or quality. It answers the question *what kind?* This type of adjective may be an **ATTRIBUTIVE** or a **PREDICATE** adjective. It may also function as a noun itself—a **SUBSTANTIVE** adjective. Descriptive adjectives may *compare* a noun's attribute—a **COMPARATIVE** adjective—and convey the highest or lowest degree of an attribute—a **SUPERLATIVE** adjective.

Attributive Descriptive Adjective

An attributive descriptive adjective *modifies* a noun, often by preceding it.

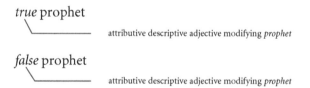

true prophet

           attributive descriptive adjective modifying *prophet*

false prophet

           attributive descriptive adjective modifying *prophet*

Predicate Descriptive Adjective

A predicate descriptive adjective makes a *comment* about a noun or pronoun. It follows a linking verb, most commonly a form of *be,* though *seem, appear, become, feel,* and *taste* are frequent.

158

The prophet's words were *true*.

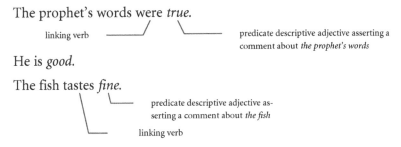

linking verb — predicate descriptive adjective asserting a comment about *the prophet's words*

He is *good*.

The fish tastes *fine*.

predicate descriptive adjective asserting a comment about *the fish*

linking verb

The Galilee sun feels *warm*.

Substantive Descriptive Adjective

A substantive descriptive adjective is one that functions as a noun. It does not modify another noun but becomes a noun in function.

> The *poor* live outside the city gate.

> The *rich* live by the temple.

> The Pharisee invited only the *wealthy*.

Comparative Descriptive Adjective

A comparative descriptive adjective expresses a greater, lesser, or equal degree of a noun's attribute. Here is how English routinely conveys comparison:

➤ Comparison of greater degree

- short adjective + *−er* + *than* + noun whose attribute is surpassed

Jerusalem is high*er than* Jericho.

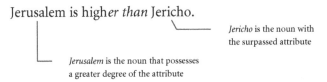

Jericho is the noun with the surpassed attribute

Jerusalem is the noun that possesses a greater degree of the attribute

Jesus is old*er than* James.

- *more* + long(er) adjective + *than* + noun whose attribute is surpassed

Jerusalem is *more* congested *than* Capernaum.

(technically a past participle functioning as an adjective)

- a form different from the base adjective

  This meal is *better* (base = "good") than the one at lunch.

➤ Comparison of lesser degree

- *not as* + adjective + *as* + noun whose attribute is unsurpassed

  Capernaum is *not as* congested *as* Jerusalem.

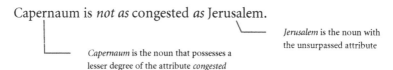

  Jerusalem is the noun with
  the unsurpassed attribute

  Capernaum is the noun that possesses a
  lesser degree of the attribute *congested*

- *less* + adjective + *than*

  The Essenes are *less* numerous *than* the Pharisees.

➤ Comparison of equal degree

- (*as* +) adjective + *as* + noun whose attribute is equaled

  Peter is (*as*) bold *as* a lion.

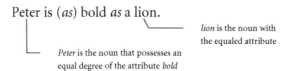

  lion is the noun with
  the equaled attribute

  Peter is the noun that possesses an
  equal degree of the attribute *bold*

Superlative Descriptive Adjective

A superlative descriptive adjective conveys the highest or lowest degree of an attribute.

➤ Superlative of highest degree

- *the* + short adjective + *–est*

  Peter is *the* bold*est* among the disciples.

- *the most* + long(er) adjective

  Judas is *the most* conniving among the disciples.

  (technically a present participle
  functioning as an adjective)

- *the* + a form different from the base adjective

  This meal is *the best* (base = "good").

➤ Superlative of lowest degree

- *the least* + adjective

  Thomas is *the least* certain.

POSSESSIVE ADJECTIVE

A possessive adjective describes or modifies a noun by stating who possesses it. The owner is the **POSSESSOR** and the modified noun is the **POSSESSED**.

	Singular	Plural
1st person	my (common)	our (common)
2d person	your (common)	your (common)
3d person	his (masculine)	their (common)
	her (feminine)	
	its (neuter)	

Figure 35: English Possessive Adjectives

A possessive adjective has only the possessor in mind, not the possessed. That is, it does not agree in gender or number with the possessed.

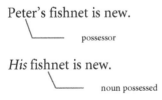

Peter's fishnet is new.

possessor

His fishnet is new.

noun possessed

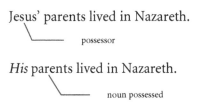

Jesus' parents lived in Nazareth.

⌐———— possessor

His parents lived in Nazareth.

⌐———— noun possessed

INTERROGATIVE ADJECTIVE

An interrogative adjective asks a question about a noun. *Which* and *what* are in-terrogative adjectives *when they are in front of the noun and ask a question.* The form never changes regardless of the syntactic function of the modified noun.

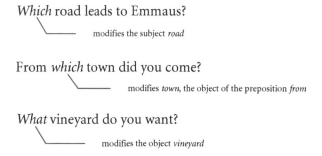

Which road leads to Emmaus?

⌐———— modifies the subject *road*

From *which* town did you come?

⌐———— modifies *town*, the object of the preposition *from*

What vineyard do you want?

⌐———— modifies the object *vineyard*

INDEFINITE ADJECTIVE

Indefinite adjectives modify nouns without regard for whether the nouns are known or identified. We can group many (but not all) of them into one primary bundle, which we can call the *many–few* (plus their relatives) bundle.

many	few
all	each
some	any
both	one
others	other/another
several	

These indefinite *adjectives* can function as *pronouns*. Don't confuse them. The lat-ter *replaces* a noun while the former *modifies* a noun, usually by standing before the noun. Here are examples of the indefinite *adjective.*

modifies the noun *people*

Many people saw the miracles.

The *other* disciples lagged behind.

As a comparison, look at the following similar sentences, which use *pronouns:*

Someone whispered to the Pharisees.

Many saw the miracles.

The *other* lagged behind.

He healed a *few.*

DEMONSTRATIVE ADJECTIVE

A demonstrative adjective points out a noun. Think of the related word *demonstrate.* The demonstrative adjective *demonstrates;* it points out. We categorize demonstrative adjectives according to whether they are NEAR (at hand) or REMOTE (farther/further away)[40] and SINGULAR or PLURAL. English makes no distinction for gender.

	Near	Remote
Singular	this	that
Plural	these	those

Figure 36: English Demonstrative Adjectives

This clay jar is Mary's but *those* jars are Martha's.

refers to one clay jar at hand   refers to many jars farther away

We make a clear distinction between demonstrative adjectives and demonstrative pronouns (see **DEMONSTRATIVE PRONOUN**, p. 127).

➢ Demonstrative adjectives stand before a noun and modify it.

---

[40] In English, we say "farther away" when *space* is in view and "further away" when *time* and other *nonspatial* relationships are in view.

This ram belongs to him.

These sheep pasture on the hill.

That goat lagged behind *those* men.

➤ Demonstrative pronouns *replace* a noun and thus do not modify one.

This is the ram.

These are the sheep on the hill.

That is the goat that lagged behind.

BIBLICAL GREEK

DESCRIPTIVE ADJECTIVE

Grammars of Biblical Greek often refer to the descriptive adjective as the POSITIVE form of the adjective, as opposed to the COMPARATIVE and SUPERLATIVE forms.

Attributive Descriptive Adjective

An attributive descriptive adjective *modifies* a noun. In Biblical Greek such an adjective can occur in four different structures/syntactic relationships. The adjective agrees with the modified noun in NUMBER, GENDER, and CASE. We need to take note of whether the structure (the adjectival *phrase*) is arthrous/articular (*with* an article) or anarthrous (with*out* an article).

Arthrous/Articular

We find three structures/syntactic relationships in arthrous/articular attributive descriptive adjectives.

➤ **Article+adjective+noun**

ὁ ἀγαθὸς ἄνθρωπος	the *good* one
the **good** person	Matthew 12:35

164

> **Article+noun+article+adjective**

τὸ φῶς τὸ **ἀληθινόν**   the *true* light

the light the **real**   John 1:9

> **Noun+article+adjective**

στολὴν τὴν **πρώτην**   the *best* robe

robe   the **foremost**   Luke 15:22

The noun in this structure is often a proper noun, a known, specific entity. As such, we can see a semantic similarity with the second format and its articular noun, which conveys a specific entity.

Ἄβελ τοῦ **δικαίου**   of *righteous* Abel

Abel   the **righteous**   Matthew 23:35

Anarthrous

> **Noun+adjective** or **adjective+noun**

κλάδους **μεγάλους**   *large* branches

branches **large**   Mark 4:32

αὐχμηρῷ τόπῳ   *dark* place

dark   place   2 Peter 1:19

Different Meanings between Attributive Adjective Structures?

One of the underpinnings of this book's investigation into languages is to assume that difference in language means difference. We assume as a starting point that different structures in a language convey different meanings. After a thorough investigation, however, we might be forced to see that two different structures do indeed have the same meaning. That is fine, of course. We simply do not *start* with that assumption. Within language, *complete* and *utter* sameness between different structures is not frequent.

As a brief case in point, in a structure where the adjective occurs before the noun, Robertson was an early voice expressing that one should see the adjective as more prominent than the noun.[41] The adjective is more informationally salient. Conversely, where the noun is before the adjective, the noun is more prominent.

Predicate Descriptive Adjective

A predicate descriptive adjective makes a *comment* about a noun or pronoun. In Biblical Greek it stands as the predicate in a *verbless* clause (see **ADJECTIVE PREDICATE**, p. 199). It also occurs in *verbal* clauses with linking verbs, similarly to English, such as εἰμί *be* and φαίνω *appear* (in middle and passive voice). The adjective agrees in **NUMBER**, **GENDER**, and **CASE** with the noun about which the adjective makes a comment. We need to take note of whether the structure in question includes an article. Regardless of whether an article is present or the clause is verbless or verbal, the basic structures/formats we encounter are these:

➤ SUBJECT (noun/pronoun) + PREDICATE (adjective), that is, S–P

➤ PREDICATE (adjective) + SUBJECT (noun/pronoun), that is, P–S

Verbless Clause

When the clause in Biblical Greek is verb*less,* to convey Biblical Greek's meaning, English commonly supplies a form of *be* or another linking verb, as we saw above. English thus expresses Greek's verbless clause with a verbal one. Biblical Greek has no linking verb in this verbless construction. The predicate adjective in a verbless clause is often simply side by side with the subject; that is, it is JUXTA-POSED.

---

[41] A. T. Robertson, *A Grammar of the Greek New Testament in the Light of Historical Research* (5th ed.; New York: Richard R. Smith; London: Hodder & Stoughton, 1931), 776: "[T]he adjective receives greater emphasis than the substantive."

> S–P

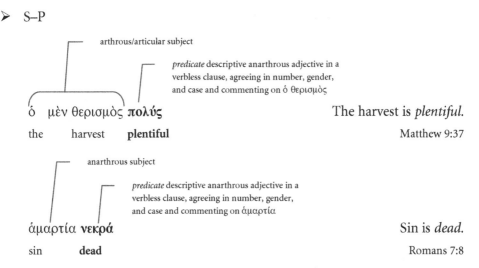

ὁ	μὲν θερισμὸς	πολύς	The harvest is *plentiful.*
the	harvest	**plentiful**	Matthew 9:37

ἁμαρτία	νεκρά	Sin is *dead.*
sin	**dead**	Romans 7:8

In the last example, with both the subject and the predicate adjective anarthrous, it is *textual environment,* that is, *textual context* that plays a very important role in understanding the structure/syntax as conveying predication or simple attribution ("sin is dead" vs. "dead sin").

> P–S

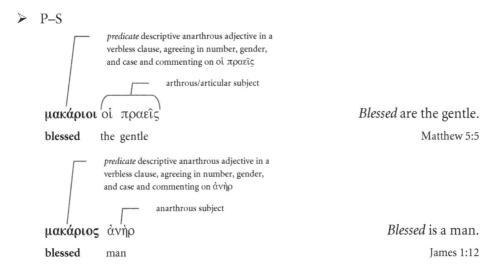

μακάριοι	οἱ πραεῖς	*Blessed* are the gentle.
blessed	the gentle	Matthew 5:5

μακάριος	ἀνὴρ	*Blessed* is a man.
blessed	man	James 1:12

In the last example, with both the subject and the predicate adjective anarthrous, it is *textual environment,* that is, *textual context* that plays a very important role in understanding the structure/syntax as conveying predication or simple attribution ("blessed is a man" vs. "blessed man").

Verbal Clause

Descriptive adjectives in Biblical Greek also occur in verbal clauses, that is, where a verb is present and an adjective is part of the predicate. The verb is commonly a form of εἰμί *be*, though other verbs occur with predicate adjectives.

➢ S–P

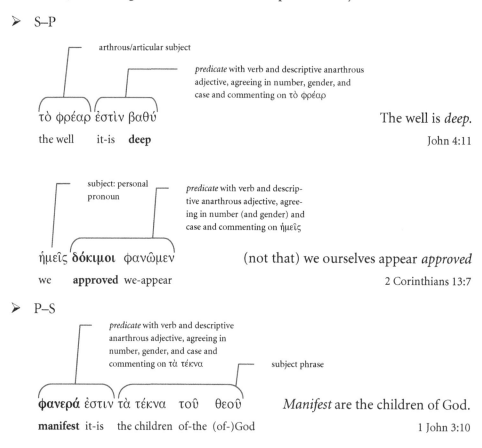

arthrous/articular subject

predicate with verb and descriptive anarthrous adjective, agreeing in number, gender, and case and commenting on τὸ φρέαρ

τὸ φρέαρ ἐστὶν βαθύ

the well   it-is   **deep**

The well is *deep*.

John 4:11

subject: personal pronoun

predicate with verb and descriptive anarthrous adjective, agreeing in number (and gender) and case and commenting on ἡμεῖς

ἡμεῖς **δόκιμοι** φανῶμεν

we   **approved** we-appear

(not that) we ourselves appear *approved*

2 Corinthians 13:7

➢ P–S

predicate with verb and descriptive anarthrous adjective, agreeing in number, gender, and case and commenting on τὰ τέκνα

subject phrase

φανερά ἐστιν τὰ τέκνα   τοῦ   θεοῦ

manifest it-is   the children of-the (of-)God

Manifest are the children of God.

1 John 3:10

Substantive Descriptive Adjective

Like English, a substantive descriptive adjective in Biblical Greek is one that functions as a noun.

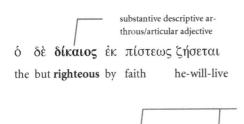

ὁ δὲ **δίκαιος** ἐκ πίστεως ζήσεται

the but **righteous** by faith   he-will-live

But the *righteous one* by faith lives.

Romans 1:17

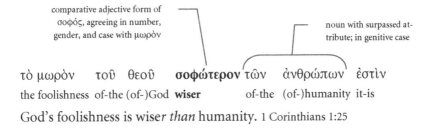

βρέχει   ἐπὶ **δικαίους** καὶ **ἀδίκους**

he-brings-rain upon **righteous** and **unjust**

He brings rain upon
righteous and *unjust.*

Matthew 5:45

Comparative Descriptive Adjective

A comparative descriptive adjective expresses a greater, lesser, or equal degree of a noun's attribute.

Biblical Greek has special forms of the adjective when it conveys comparison. The forms below represent the bulk of what we find in Biblical Greek.

➤ Comparison of greater degree

- stem of adjective + –τερος (inflected for gender, number, case) + noun/pronoun in genitive case

comparative adjective form of
σοφός, agreeing in number,
gender, and case with μωρὸν

noun with surpassed at-
tribute; in genitive case

τὸ μωρὸν   τοῦ θεοῦ   **σοφώτερον** τῶν   ἀνθρώπων   ἐστὶν

the foolishness of-the (of-)God **wiser**   of-the (of-)humanity it-is

God's foolishness is wise*r than* humanity. 1 Corinthians 1:25

- a different form from the positive adjective + –(ι)ων (inflected for gender, number, case) + noun/pronoun in genitive case

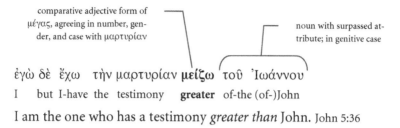

comparative adjective form of
μέγας, agreeing in number, gender, and case with μαρτυρίαν

noun with surpassed attribute; in genitive case

ἐγὼ δὲ ἔχω τὴν μαρτυρίαν **μείζω** τοῦ Ἰωάννου
I but I-have the testimony **greater** of-the (of-)John

I am the one who has a testimony *greater than* John. John 5:36

> Comparison of equal degree

- adjective + comparative particle

γίνεσθε οὖν **φρόνιμοι ὡς** οἱ ὄφεις   Be *as wise as* serpents!
be   therefore **wise**   **as** the serpents   Matthew 10:16

Superlative Descriptive Adjective

A superlative descriptive adjective conveys the highest or lowest degree of an attribute.

Biblical Greek has special forms of the adjective when it conveys the superlative. The forms below represent the bulk of what we find in Biblical Greek.

> Superlative of highest degree

- stem of adjective + –τατος (inflected for gender, number, case)

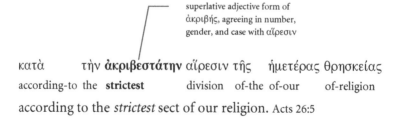

superlative adjective form of
ἀκριβής, agreeing in number, gender, and case with αἵρεσιν

κατὰ   τὴν **ἀκριβεστάτην** αἵρεσιν τῆς   ἡμετέρας θρησκείας
according-to the **strictest**   division of-the of-our   of-religion

according to the *strictest* sect of our religion. Acts 26:5

170

- a different form from the positive adjective + –ιστος (inflected for gender, number, case)

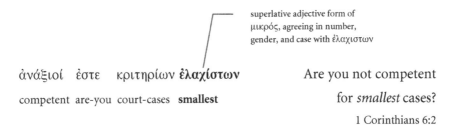

superlative adjective form of
μικρός, agreeing in number,
gender, and case with ἐλαχίστων

ἀνάξιοί ἐστε κριτηρίων **ἐλαχίστων**   Are you not competent

competent are-you court-cases **smallest**   for *smallest* cases?

1 Corinthians 6:2

Excursus: Semantic Shifts in Biblical Greek Descriptive Adjectives

Whatever the underlying causes, we witness, in Biblical Greek, shifts in meaning between positive, comparative, and superlative descriptive adjectives. We see, additionally, the use of what grammars call the ELATIVE.[42] This refers to, for want of a better description, the *elation* of an attribute conveyed by a descriptive adjective form. The elative of the attribute *happy*, for example, could be expressed in English as **very happy**. More advanced grammars discuss and cite many examples. One can find instances of

- the positive expressing the comparative,

- the positive expressing the superlative,

- the comparative expressing the positive,

- the comparative expressing the superlative,

- the comparative expressing the elative,

- the superlative expressing the comparative,

- the superlative expressing the elative, etc.[43]

---

[42] *Elative* in linguistics more commonly refers to a particular grammatical case that expresses motion "away from (inside)." It is used in Finnish, for example.

[43] For example, see discussions in such grammars as Robertson, *Grammar,* 659–671; Nigel Turner, *Syntax,* 29–32; Wallace, *Greek Grammar,* 296–305.

POSSESSIVE ADJECTIVE

A possessive adjective describes or modifies a noun by stating who possesses it.
The owner is the POSSESSOR and the modified noun is the POSSESSED.

possessive adjective in article + adjective + noun attributive syntax

ὅτι   ὁ **ἐμὸς** καιρὸς οὔπω πεπλήρωται   Because *my* time is not yet

because the **my**   time   not-yet he-is-fulfilled   fully come.

John 7:8

possessive adjective in article + adjective + noun attributive syntax

οὐ τῷ   **σῷ**   ὀνόματι ἐπροφητεύσαμεν Did we not prophesy in *your* name?

not in-the (**in-**)**your** name   we-prophesied   Matthew 7:22

possessive adjective in article + noun + article + adjective attributive syntax

ἡ κρίσις ἡ **ἐμὴ** δικαία ἐστίν   *My* judgment is just.

the judgment the **my** upright she-is   John 5:30

possessive adjective in noun + article + adjective attributive syntax

εἰρήνην τὴν **ἐμὴν** δίδωμι ὑμῖν   *My* peace I give to you.

peace   the **my** I-give to-you   John 14:27

In the chart of forms below, do not forget that the *persons* are singular or plural,
but the noun being modified by the possessive adjective might be either singular
or plural. Thus you will see room for two forms for every grammatical case: one
for when the modified noun is singular; one for when it is plural.

			Singular			Plural		
			masc	fem	neuter	masc	fem	neuter
1st person	nom	s	ἐμός	ἐμή	ἐμόν	—	ἡμέτερα	—
		pl	ἐμοί	—	ἐμά	ἡμέτεροι	—	—
	acc	s	ἐμόν	ἐμήν	ἐμόν	—	ἡμετέραν	—
		pl	ἐμούς	ἐμάς	ἐμά	—	—	—
	gen	s	—	ἐμῆς	ἐμοῦ	—	ἡμετέρας	—
		pl	—	—	ἐμῶν	—	ἡμετέρων	—
	dat	s	ἐμῷ	ἐμῇ	ἐμῷ	—	—	—
		pl	—	—	ἐμοῖς	ἡμετέροις	ἡμετέραις	—
			the person speaking			the person speaking + others		
2d person	nom	s	σός	—	σόν	ὑμέτερος	ὑμέτερα[44]	—
		pl	σοί	—	σά	—	—	—
	acc	s	—	σήν	σόν	ὑμέτερον	ὑμετέραν	ὑμέτερον
		pl	σούς	—	σά	—	—	—
	gen	s	—	σῆς	—	—	ὑμετέρας	—
		pl	—	—	—	—	—	—
	dat	s	σῷ	σῇ	σῷ	ὑμετέρῳ	ὑμετέρα	ὑμετέρῳ
		pl	—	—	—	—	—	—
			the person spoken to			the persons spoken to		
3d person	nom	s	ἴδιος	—	—	—	—	—
		pl	ἴδιοι	—	ἴδια	—	—	—
	acc	s	ἴδιον	ἰδίαν	ἴδιον	—	—	—
		pl	ἰδίους	ἰδίας	ἴδια	—	—	—
	gen	s	ἰδίου	ἰδίας	ἰδίου	—	—	—
		pl	ἰδίων	ἰδίων	ἰδίων	—	—	—
	dat	s	ἰδίῳ	ἰδίᾳ	ἰδίῳ	—	—	—
		pl	ἰδίοις	ἰδίαις	ἰδίοις	—	—	—
			the entity spoken about			the entities spoken about		

Figure 37: Biblical Greek Possessive Adjectives

[44] This form is used only as a possessive *pronoun*. See the example on p. 140 under POSSESSIVE PRONOUN.

INTERROGATIVE ADJECTIVE

An interrogative adjective asks a question about a noun. Biblical Greek's inventory of this kind of adjective leads us to see that it includes three major types. (1) One type asks for or seeks out IDENTITY, that is, "what?" (2) Another asks for QUALITY, "what sort?" or "what kind?" (3) The third asks for QUANTITY, "how many?" or "how much?"

Keep in mind that many Biblical Greek grammars talk only of interrogative *pronouns*. The grammars might or might not mention that these "pronouns" can function as adjectives. The label *interrogative pronoun* does not always correctly describe the interrogative's precise function in a text. When an interrogative pronoun is truly a pronoun, then the label fits. When an interrogative "pronoun" functions as an adjective, we ought to understand it as an "interrogative adjective."

This section treats *only* the interrogative "pronoun" when it functions as an *adjective*. A "true" interrogative adjective is one that *modifies* a nominal; it does not replace it: "*What* reward will you receive?" or "*Which* house is Peter's?"

Do not hesitate to compare this section with the one entitled INTERROGATIVE PRONOUN, pp. 124, 140.

Interrogative Adjective for IDENTITY

τίς, as an adjective, will commonly be translated "what?" when it refers to a masculine or feminine grammatical entity that to an English speaker is inanimate.

τί	ἀγαθὸν ποιήσω	*What* good thing shall I do?
what	good I-do	Matthew 19:16

Interrogative Adjective for QUALITY

A few interrogative adjectives ask "what sort?" or "what kind?" They are τίς/τί, ποῖος, and ποταπός.

> τίς (in accusative case), from *textual environment,* is
> most likely asking for *quality* and not simply identity

τίνα μισθὸν ἔχετε

what reward have-you

What(kind of) reward do you have?

Matthew 5:46

ποῖον οἶκον οἰκοδομήσετέ μοι

what-kind-of house will-you-build for-me

What kind of house will you build for me?

Acts 7:49

ποταπός ἐστιν οὗτος

what-sort is-he this

What kind of man is this one?

Matthew 8:27

Interrogative Adjective for QUANTITY

One interrogative adjective asks "how many?" or "how much?" It is πόσος.

πόσους ἔχετε ἄρτους

how-many have-you loaves

How many loaves do you have?

Mark 8:5

A chart of the forms of τίς/τί is on p. 143 under **INTERROGATIVE PRONOUN**.

INDEFINITE ADJECTIVE

Indefinite adjectives modify nouns without regard for whether the nouns are known or identified. In Biblical Greek we account for NUMBER (singular and plural), GENDER, and CASE. The indefinite adjective's form is identical to the interrogative's, apart from the accents. Do not confuse an indefinite *adjective* with an indefinite *pronoun* (see **INDEFINITE PRONOUN**, pp. 126, 143). The latter *replaces* a noun while the former modifies a noun.

ἐγένετο ... ἱερεύς **τις**

it-was priest **a**

There was ... *a certain* priest.

Luke 1:5

ἐὰν γένηταί **τινι** ἀνθρώπῳ ἑκατὸν πρόβατα   if *a* person has a

if   he-has   **a**   person   100   sheep   hundred sheep

Matthew 18:12

A chart of the forms of τις/τι is on p. 144 under **INDEFINITE PRONOUN**.

DEMONSTRATIVE ADJECTIVE

Grammars regularly talk of the Biblical Greek demonstratives as modifying nouns—demonstrative *adjectives*. The structure/syntax, however, is described as being *predicate adjective*. Such demonstratives do *not* occur in an "attributive adjective" structure/syntax, which we would expect.

Consult **EXCURSUS: ON THE STRUCTURE/SYNTAX OF DEMONSTRATIVES**, p. 146, which takes you through the issues and, in the end, argues that we might be better advised to talk of the demonstrative functioning as a *pronoun* in a structure/syntax known as **APPOSITION**. Thus *this book* does not talk of demonstratives being adjectives, but you should recognize that many grammars do.

ADVERB

An **ADVERB** is commonly a word that modifies or describes a verb, an adjective, or another adverb. Adverbs convey such concepts as time, place, quantity, manner, and intensity.

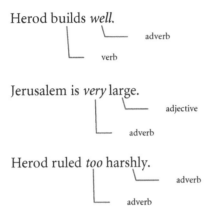

Herod builds *well.*
        adverb
      verb

Jerusalem is *very* large.
      adjective
      adverb

Herod ruled *too* harshly.
      adverb
      adverb

An **ADVERB** or **ADVERBIAL** can also refer to all components of language connected to the verb. This is a broad use of the term, and usually *ADVERBIAL* is the preferred label for this wide use. I explore this in detail under the chapter **PREDICATE/PREDICATION**, particularly under **VERBAL PREDICATION**, p. 201.

ENGLISH

➤ adverbs of **TIME** address the issue of *when*

The orphans arrived *early.*

The ship arrived *late* in Caesarea.

➤ adverbs of **PLACE** address the issue of *where*

The orphans were left *behind.*

Paul looked *around.*

➢ adverbs of **QUANTITY** address the issue *how much* or *how well*

The top of Mt. Hermon is *very* cold.

Mary eats *little*.

➢ adverbs of **MANNER** address the issue of *how*. Many of them are formed by adding *–ly* to a base form of the adjective.

They walked along the path *carefully*.

The daughters of Jerusalem danced *beautifully*.

➢ adverbs of **INTENSITY** address emphasis

Herod was a *really* shrewd ruler.

Thomas did *actually* doubt the report.

➢ adverbs of **CAUSE** or **PURPOSE** address the issue of *why, what for*

I will *therefore* refuse to pay homage!

Some adverbs in English are precisely the same form as their adjective counterparts. Remember that adverbs modify verbs, adjectives, and other adverbs whereas adjectives modify nouns and pronouns.

Adverb	**Adjective**
The ship sailed *fast*.	The *fast* ship arrived.
I *only* drink wine.	Masada was the *only* community left.
They work *hard*.	That was *hard* work.

BIBLICAL GREEK

Here are but a few of many semantic categories.

➢ adverbs of **TIME** address the issue of *when*

τότε ἐξεπορεύετο πρὸς αὐτὸν Ἱεροσόλυμα

then it-was-going-out to him Jerusalem

At that time Jerusalem was going out to him.

Matthew 3:5

178

➤ adverbs of PLACE address the issue of *where*

ἴσθι   ἐκεῖ   Remain *there!*

remain **there**   Matthew 2:13

➤ adverbs of MANNER address the issue of *how*

καταμάθετε τὰ κρίνα   τοῦ ἀγροῦ **πῶς** αὐξάνουσιν

consider   the wild-flowers of-the countryside **how** they-spread

Consider *how* the wild flowers of the countryside grow. Matthew 6:28

➤ adverbs of INTENSITY address emphasis

ἐξεπλήσσοντο   **σφόδρα**   They were *very* astonished.

they-were-astonished **greatly**   Matthew 19:25

BROAD USE OF THE TERM ADVERBIAL

I mentioned above that the term *adverbial* could refer to any component of language connected to the verb. Dividing adverbials into two main categories is helpful: (1) ADVERBIAL COMPLEMENT and (2) ADVERBIAL ADJUNCT. I discuss this in detail under the section VERBAL PREDICATION (see p. 201) in the chapter PREDICATE/PREDICATION.

PARTICIPLE

A **PARTICIPLE** is a word form that *participates* in the world of the verb and the world of the nominal. It can function as a verb and as an adjective.

ENGLISH

The participle in English has

➤ tense: *present* or *past* (see **TENSE**, p. 60);

➤ voice: *active, middle,* or *passive* (see **VOICE**, p. 98).

The **PRESENT PARTICIPLE** ends in *-ing*: eat*ing*, rid*ing*, writ*ing*.

The **PAST PARTICIPLE** is the form we use after *He has: He has **eaten, ridden, written**.* We form the past participle usually by adding *-ed, -d, -t,* or *-en* to the dictionary form of the verb.

Participles have two main functions in English: (1) **VERBAL FORMS (TO CREATE TENSE)** and (2) **ADJECTIVES**.

VERBAL FORMS

Used in combination with an auxiliary verb, participles form several tenses (see the discussion of **TENSE** for English, p. 60).

Present Participle

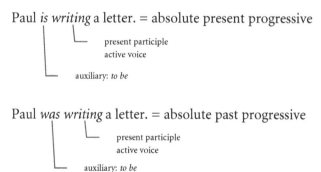

Paul *is writing* a letter. = absolute present progressive
- present participle
- active voice
- auxiliary: *to be*

Paul *was writing* a letter. = absolute past progressive
- present participle
- active voice
- auxiliary: *to be*

Paul *has been writing* a letter. = present perfect progressive

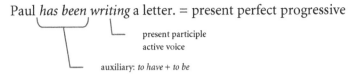

- present participle
  active voice

auxiliary: *to have + to be*

Past Participle

With the auxiliary verb *to have*, the past participle forms tense. With the auxiliary verb *to be*, the past participle assists in conveying the passive voice.

Paul *has written* a letter. = present perfect (active voice)

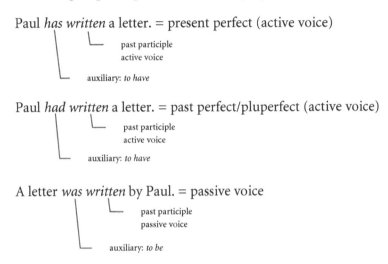

- past participle
  active voice

auxiliary: *to have*

Paul *had written* a letter. = past perfect/pluperfect (active voice)

- past participle
  active voice

auxiliary: *to have*

A letter *was written* by Paul. = passive voice

- past participle
  passive voice

auxiliary: *to be*

ADJECTIVES

Functioning as adjectives, participles can

➢ occur as a *single word* modifying a nominal

➢ or initiate a *participial phrase* that modifies a nominal.

Single Word

In this function, the participle behaves very much in the world of the nominal with little view toward a verbal process (in comparison with situations where it begins a participial phrase). This function in English is akin to what is commonly called the **ADJECTIVAL PARTICIPLE** in Biblical Greek (see p. 184).

Attributive Adjective

A word is *modified* by a participle functioning as an adjective.

Peter was an *amazing* disciple.

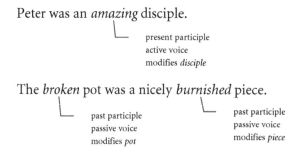

present participle
active voice
modifies *disciple*

The *broken* pot was a nicely *burnished* piece.

past participle
passive voice
modifies *pot*

past participle
passive voice
modifies *piece*

Predicate Adjective

A participle functioning as an adjective makes a *comment* on a word with the help of a linking verb.

Peter was *amazing*.

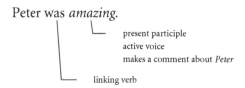

present participle
active voice
makes a comment about *Peter*

linking verb

Substantive Adjective

A participle functions as a noun/substantive.

Jesus talked to the *amazed*.

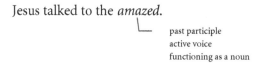

past participle
active voice
functioning as a noun

Participial Phrase

The participial phrase modifies a nominal outside the phrase.

In this function, the participle behaves very much in the world of the verb; the phrase usually conveys a verbal process. This function in English is comparable to what is commonly called the VERBAL PARTICIPLE in Biblical Greek (see p. 185).

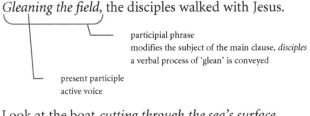

Gleaning the field, the disciples walked with Jesus.

participial phrase
modifies the subject of the main clause, *disciples*
a verbal process of 'glean' is conveyed

present participle
active voice

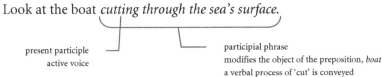

Look at the boat *cutting through the sea's surface.*

present participle
active voice

participial phrase
modifies the object of the preposition, *boat*
a verbal process of 'cut' is conveyed

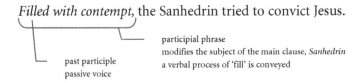

Filled with contempt, the Sanhedrin tried to convict Jesus.

participial phrase
modifies the subject of the main clause, *Sanhedrin*
a verbal process of 'fill' is conveyed

past participle
passive voice

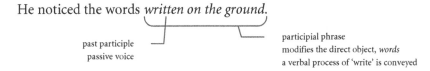

He noticed the words *written on the ground.*

past participle
passive voice

participial phrase
modifies the direct object, *words*
a verbal process of 'write' is conveyed

BIBLICAL GREEK

The participle in Biblical Greek has

➢ aspect (see TENSE AND ASPECT, p. 60), occurring in the present, aorist, perfect, and future "tense"-forms;

➢ voice: *active, middle(–reflexive),* and *passive* (see VOICE, p. 98);

➢ case (see p. 34), number (see p. 32), and gender (see p. 30).

The participle focuses more on the *participant* related to the verbal process associated with the participle. This, in part, explains why a participle inflects for the number and gender of the words to which it is closely connected.

The other nonfinite verb form (see FINITE AND NONFINITE, p. 57) in Biblical Greek, the INFINITIVE (p. 187), focuses more on the *process* and thus occurs without number and case and in only one gender.

We shall consider two primary functions of the participle in Biblical Greek. They are (1) the ADJECTIVAL PARTICIPLE and (2) the VERBAL PARTICIPLE.

ADJECTIVAL PARTICIPLE

Similarly to English, Biblical Greek participles have three common adjectival functions.

Attributive Adjective

A word is *modified* by a participle functioning as an adjective.

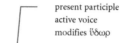

present participle
active voice
modifies ὕδωρ

πόθεν   οὖν ἔχεις τὸ ὕδωρ **τὸ ζῶν** Where then do you get the *living* water?

from-where then get-you the water **the living**   John 4:11

Predicate Adjective

A participle functioning as an adjective makes a *comment* on a word.

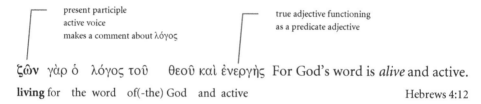

present participle
active voice
makes a comment about λόγος

true adjective functioning
as a predicate adjective

ζῶν γὰρ ὁ λόγος τοῦ   θεοῦ καὶ ἐνεργὴς For God's word is *alive* and active.

living for   the word of(-the) God   and active   Hebrews 4:12

Substantive Adjective

The participle functions as a noun/substantive.

ὁ ποιήσας τὸ ἔλεος μετ'   αὐτοῦ   *the one who showed* mercy toward him

the doing-one the mercy toward him   Luke 10:37

μακαρία **ἡ πιστεύσασα**   Blessed is *she who believed*.

blessed **the believed/believer**   Luke 1:45

VERBAL PARTICIPLE

Participles convey a verbal process even when they are functioning primarily as adjectives. Compare, for example, these two phrases: (1) *the red book;* (2) *the written book.* The first uses a true attributive descriptive adjective; the second, a participle. Notice how the participle *written* conveys a verbal process ('write') that *red* simply does not have.

In the VERBAL PARTICIPLE the verbal process of a participle is *particularly* salient, more so than in the adjective participle. A verbal participle conveys a verbal process. In Biblical Greek a verbal participle is most commonly dependent on a *controlling* or *head* entity or verbal process (often) in a main clause.

A host of meaningful connections link the verbal participle to its head: time, manner (*He came **trembling***), means (*We speak by **using** our mouths*), cause, etc. An advanced grammar will steer you through them.

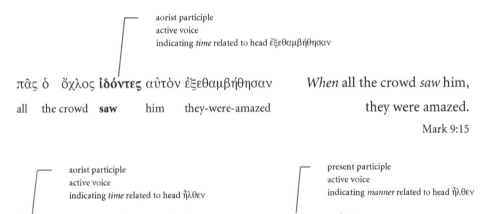

aorist participle
active voice
indicating *time* related to head ἐξεθαμβήθησαν

πᾶς ὁ ὄχλος **ἰδόντες** αὐτὸν ἐξεθαμβήθησαν
all the crowd **saw** him they-were-amazed

When all the crowd *saw* him,
they were amazed.

Mark 9:15

aorist participle
active voice
indicating *time* related to head ἦλθεν

present participle
active voice
indicating *manner* related to head ἦλθεν

ἰδοῦσα δὲ ἡ γυνὴ ὅτι οὐκ ἔλαθεν **τρέμουσα** ἦλθεν
saw now the woman that not she-escaped-notice **trembling** she-came

Now *when* the woman *had seen* that she hadn't escaped notice, she came *trembling.* Luke 8:47

185

present participle
middle voice
indicating *means* related to head κοπιῶμεν

κοπιῶμεν **ἐργαζόμενοι** ταῖς ἰδίαις χερσίν

we-labor **working** the own hands

We labor, *by working* with our own hands.

1 Corinthians 4:12

186

INFINITIVE

An **INFINITIVE** is a verbal noun (part verb, part noun) and a nonfinite verb form (for a definition see **FINITE AND NONFINITE**, p. 57, under **VERB**). It focuses on the *process* involved with the verb. In many languages, the infinitive is the *base* or *dictionary* form.

ENGLISH

The infinitive is the dictionary form of the verb: *walk, see, read,* etc. The infinitive is often used along with the main verb. We commonly attach *to* to the infinitive.

An infinitive, as part verb, conveys a verbal process. As part noun, it can fill most any syntactic slot in a clause (subject, adverbial, etc.). An infinitive or infinitive clause can, for example, be the following:

➢ **SUBJECT** of a larger clause:

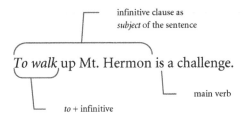

➢ **PREDICATE (NOMINATIVE)** of a clause with the verb *be:*

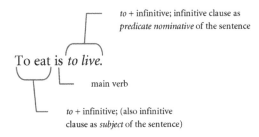

187

> ➤ ADVERBIAL COMPLEMENT (see p. 196) of a larger verbal clause:

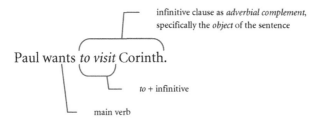

> ➤ or ADVERBIAL ADJUNCT (see p. 197) of a larger verbal clause:

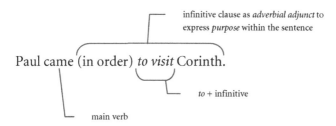

With some verbs, such as *let* and *must,* we use the infinitive without *to.*

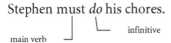

BIBLICAL GREEK

The infinitive in Biblical Greek is *not* the base or dictionary form. It is a specially marked form. The other nonfinite verb form, the PARTICIPLE (see p. 180), focuses more on the *participant* of the verbal process. This, in part, explains why participles inflect for number, gender, and case. Infinitives, which focus more on the *process* of a verbal process, do not themselves indicate number or case, and occur in only one gender.

As in English, an infinitive, as part verb, conveys a verbal process. As part noun, it can fill most any syntactic slot in a clause (subject, adverbial, etc.). An infinitive or infinitive clause can, for example, be the following:

➢ **SUBJECT** of a larger clause:

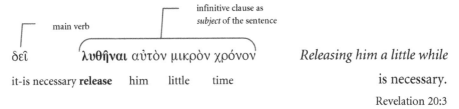

➢ **ADVERBIAL COMPLEMENT** (see p. 196) of a larger clause:

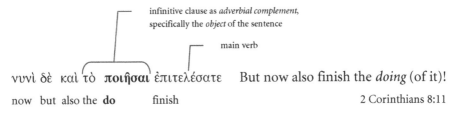

➢ **ADVERBIAL ADJUNCT** (see p. 197) of a larger clause:

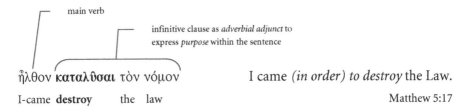

Part III

The Clause and Beyond

CLAUSE

A CLAUSE is a language unit referring to a string of words (a SYNTAGM) that involves a COMMENT, very commonly about a subject that is *usually* present. (Infinitive clauses are noteworthy for often not having an explicit subject.) The comment is known as the PREDICATE. We commonly talk of two foremost types of clauses: (1) INDEPENDENT and MAIN and (2) DEPENDENT or SUBORDINATE.

INDEPENDENT AND MAIN

A clause that stands on its own, with its own complete thought, is an independent clause. The terms *independent* and *main* are not completely synonymous. When an independent clause has a dependent or subordinate clause linked to it, we use *main* to refer to it. An *independent* clause has no dependent/subordinate clause linked to it.

ENGLISH

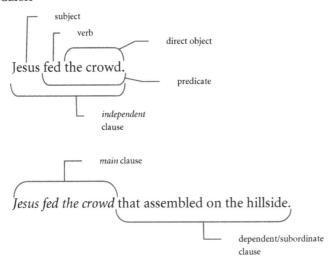

BIBLICAL GREEK

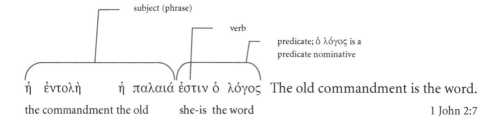

ἡ ἐντολὴ ἡ παλαιά ἐστιν ὁ λόγος   The old commandment is the word.
the commandment the old   she-is the word   1 John 2:7

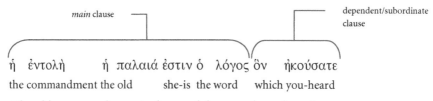

ἡ ἐντολὴ ἡ παλαιά ἐστιν ὁ λόγος ὃν ἠκούσατε
the commandment the old   she-is the word which you-heard

The old commandment is the word that you have heard. 1 John 2:7

DEPENDENT OR SUBORDINATE

A clause that does not stand on its own and must be linked to a main clause is a dependent or subordinate clause. The terms *dependent* and *subordinate* are quite synonymous, unlike *independent* and *main*.

ENGLISH

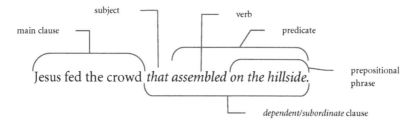

194

BIBLICAL GREEK

```
                                              ┌──────── direct object
                  main clause ──┐             │
                                │        ┌─────┴─── dependent/subordinate
                                │        │         clause
       ╭──────────────╮  ╭──────┴───────╮╭┴──────────╮
       ἡ  ἐντολὴ        ἡ  παλαιά ἐστιν ὁ λόγος   ὃν   ἠκούσατε
       the commandment the old    she-is the word which you-heard
```

The old commandment is the word *that you have heard.* 1 John 2:7

ANATOMY OF A VERBAL CLAUSE

In Biblical Greek a clause with verbal predication has a SUBJECT and a PREDICATE. The predicate has a VERB and may have ADVERBIALS.

Some linguists distinguish between adverbials that are *complements* (in a sense of *"complete*-ment") and those that are *adjuncts*. The former refers to a *necessary* constituent (one needed for completeness); the latter, an *unnecessary* or *optional* one.[45]

Dividing adverbials into two main categories is helpful: (1) ADVERBIAL COMPLEMENT and (2) ADVERBIAL ADJUNCT, often called the ADVERBIAL MODIFIER. One particular adverbial complement that involves the accusative case in Biblical Greek is the COMPLEMENT ACCUSATIVE. One particular adverbial adjunct subcategory that involves the accusative is the ADVERBIAL ADJUNCT ACCUSATIVE.

Here is an illustration of the major, *basic* elements of a verbal clause in Biblical Greek.

---

[45] John Lyons, *Introduction to Theoretical Linguistics* (Cambridge: Cambridge University Press, 1968), 43–50.

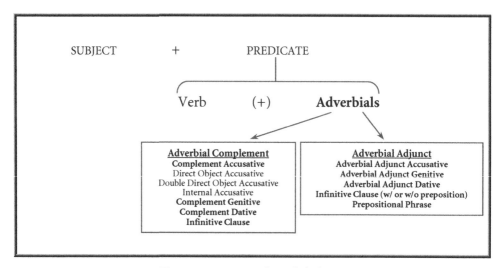

Figure 38: Anatomy of a Verbal Clause

The important point here is that a verbal clause has

➢ a **SUBJECT** (see p. 198) and **PREDICATE** (p. 199);

➢ the predicate has a **VERB** (p. 57);

➢ the verb may govern **ADVERBIALS**, either **ADVERBIAL COMPLEMENTS** or **AD-VERBIAL ADJUNCTS**.

The chapter on **CASE** in Biblical Greek (p. 36) treats the concepts of **ADVERBIAL COMPLEMENT** and **ADVERBIAL ADJUNCT** fused with case. Go there to get a full treatment. Below is simply a brief comment on each of them.

ADVERBIAL COMPLEMENT

With the ideas of *complement* and *adjunct* in mind, we say that adverbial complements are directly governed by verbs. Verbs can govern **OBJECTS**. The objects are *complements;* that is, when they occur, they *complete* the verbal process. They are necessary, needed for wholeness.

Syntactically we call them *objects. Semantically* they can stand in a variety of roles related to the verbal process: for example, **MATERIAL** = **DOING** ("Herod *killed **the*** *boys*"); MENTAL = SENSING ("He *heard **the cries**"). (See the discussion under SE-MANTICS: PROCESSES, ROLES, AND CIRCUMSTANCES, p. 203.)

ADVERBIAL ADJUNCT

With the ideas of *complement* and *adjunct* in mind, we say that adverbial adjuncts are indirectly governed by verbs and refer to *circumstances* associated with the verbal process. The dative case and prepositional phrases play a large role as adverbial adjuncts in addition to the adverbial adjunct accusative.

SUBJECT

A SUBJECT is a label for a grammatical function traditionally associated with the entity that carries out the process of a verb or about which a comment is made.

ENGLISH

To find the subject of a clause, look for a verb and ask *who?* or *what?* before saying the verb. The answer is the clause's subject.

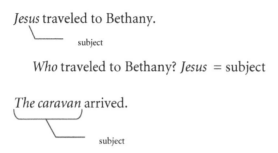

Jesus traveled to Bethany.

subject

Who traveled to Bethany? *Jesus* = subject

The caravan arrived.

subject

What arrived? *The caravan* = subject

BIBLICAL GREEK

As a rule, the subject behaves the same way in Biblical Greek as it does in English. Keep in mind:

➢ The subject is already a part of the verbal "tense"-forms. A separate word functioning as subject is not always necessary.

➢ Greek has clauses that are verbless, and both a subject and a predicate may be in the nominative case. As a *general* rule, the element that appears to be *more specific, more specified* tends to be identified as a subject. This still does not make the choice clear at times, but it appears to be a good rule of thumb. (See the discussion that begins on p. 40 under the subsection PREDICATE NOMINATIVE in the chapter on CASE.)

PREDICATE/PREDICATION

We can view a clause as having two primary components: a subject (S) and a PREDICATE (P). In English, the predicate has a verb and may have other words related to the verb, what we call ADVERBIALS (see ADVERB, p. 177, and the discussion below in this chapter under VERBAL PREDICATION).

VERBLESS and VERBAL predication are the two options for predication in Biblical Greek.

VERBLESS PREDICATION

For verbless predication, Biblical Greek uses *no finite verbal form* (for a definition of *finite*, see under VERB, p. 57) in the clause. Verbless predication is expressed most commonly by nominals (see NOMINAL, p. 118) simply sitting side by side. The concept of nominals sitting side by side is odd to English speakers because English commonly uses *linking verbs*.

(English does, however, have a construction similar to the Greek. Think of knocking on a door with the intent of finding whether anybody is present on the other side of the door. *You there?* is a verbless clause variant of *You are there?/Are you there?* which uses a linking verb, *are*.)

ADJECTIVE PREDICATE

An adjective can stand as the predicate in a verbless clause. The adjective is known as a PREDICATE (DESCRIPTIVE) ADJECTIVE. The adjective agrees in NUMBER, GENDER, and CASE with the noun about which the adjective makes a comment. We need to take note of whether the structure in question includes an article. The predicate (descriptive) adjective is treated in detail under the chapter ADJECTIVE at the subsection PREDICATE DESCRIPTIVE ADJECTIVE, p. 166. Go there to read about this type of verbless predication.

ADVERB(IAL) PREDICATE

A *prepositional phrase* or *locative adverb* (one that points to a *location*) can stand as the predicate in a verbless clause. One view of prepositions is to regard them as

nominals used *ad-verbally*. Some grammarians have thus categorized prepositional phrases, when used in verbless clauses, as adverb(ial phrase) predicates.

➤ prepositional phrase

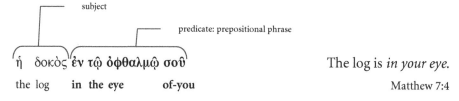

The log is *in your eye*.

Matthew 7:4

➤ locative (location) adverb

Here is the Christ/Messiah.

Matthew 24:23

SUBSTANTIVE PREDICATE

Two nouns/substantives (or phrases including nouns/substantives) or a
noun/substantive and pronoun can stand side by side to indicate predication.
When the predicate is a noun/substantive or noun/substantival phrase, this is a
substantive predicate. Examples include the following:

➤ substantive (or substantival phrase) juxtaposed to a substantive (or substantival phrase):

Spirit is God.

John 4:24

➤ substantive (or substantival phrase) juxtaposed to a pronoun:

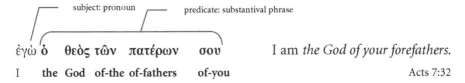

ἐγώ ὁ   θεὸς τῶν πατέρων   σου   I am *the God of your forefathers.*
I   the God of-the of-fathers of-you   Acts 7:32

VERBAL PREDICATION

In Biblical Greek expect a clause with verbal predication to have a subject and a predicate. The predicate has a verb and may have ADVERBIALS. The chapter on CASE in Biblical Greek (beginning on p. 36) explores *in depth* how case and verbal predication are intertwined. You will also want to read the section ANATOMY OF A VERBAL CLAUSE, p. 195. The intent of the present section is to focus on the big picture, the major building blocks, without offering again the particulars you will find in the CASE chapter. Everything I discuss below is developed in greater detail in that chapter.

We first need to separate out verbal predication including the nominative case from the other three (sometimes called the OBLIQUE cases). In a verbal clause, the predicate can be in the nominative case—a PREDICATE NOMINATIVE. The verbal process is most commonly conveyed through εἰμί *be, exist,* γίνομαι *become,* and ὑπάρχω *be, be at one's disposal.* The PREDICATE in this structure is frequently relationally linked to the subject, often *descriptively* (= conveying an attribute) or *equatively* (= equal), and it shares the subject's nominative case. This is a predicate nominative—the *predicate* is in the *nominative case.*

For the oblique cases, we need to distinguish between adverbials that are *complements* (in a sense of *"complete-*ment") and those that are *adjuncts.* The former term refers to a *necessary* constituent (one needed for completeness); the latter, an *unnecessary* or *optional* one.

Dividing adverbials into two main categories is helpful: (1) ADVERBIAL COMPLEMENT and (2) ADVERBIAL ADJUNCT, often called the ADVERBIAL MODIFIER. Each of the oblique cases may function in either of these two roles, as you will see in figure 39 below. For example, under *adverbial complement* you will notice a *com-*

201

plement accusative; under *adverbial adjunct,* an *adverbial adjunct accusative.* The same holds for the genitive and dative. Additionally, notice that a prepositional phrase, cast in the appropriate case according to the preposition, can be syntactically an *adverbial adjunct.*

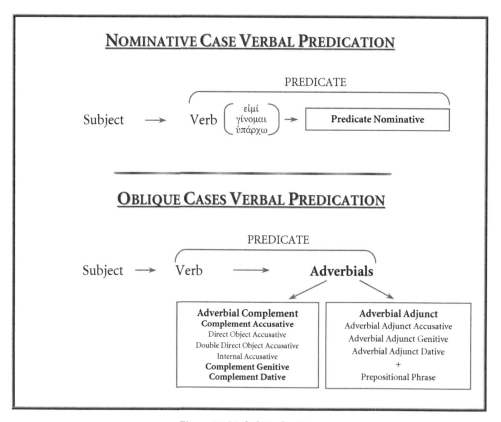

Figure 39: Verbal Predication

SEMANTICS:
PROCESSES, ROLES, AND CIRCUMSTANCES

We use language to talk about the real world. Stop and think about it. Most everything we experience and understand about the phenomena of our existence we can represent in language, in its linguistic structures. The *semantic* concepts of **PROCESS, ROLE,** and **CIRCUMSTANCE** are categories we can use to help us see how the stuff of the real world meshes with language.[46]

By *process* we refer primarily to **VERBS.**

By *role* we refer primarily to **NOUNS/NOMINALS.**

By *circumstance* we refer primarily to **ADVERB(IAL)S** and **PREPOSITIONAL PHRASES.**

SEMANTIC PROCESSES

Though we can talk of others, we shall restrict ourselves to three *primary* semantic processes: (1) material, (2) mental, and (3) relational.

MATERIAL = DOING

The **MATERIAL** semantic process is the verbal process of **DOING.** Here a *"do-er"* has an impact on a *"do-ee,"* so to speak. Quite often, the do-er is called the **AGENT** and the do-ee, the **PATIENT.** We can, however, be a little more precise. The *impact* a do-er can have is twofold.

➢ **AFFECTOR—AFFECTED**

The do-er can **AFFECT** a do-ee. The do-er is the **AFFECTOR;** the do-ee is the **AFFECTED.** The affector and affected exist, and the affector is the catalyst of an action that *affects* the existing affected.

---

[46] For further reading, see M. A. K. Halliday, *An Introduction to Functional Grammar* (2d ed.; London: Arnold, 1994), 109–60.

He hit *the idol.*

Affector *(He)* — Affected *(the idol)*

Both affector and affected already exist at the time of the verbal process, the hitting. The affector is the catalyst of the hitting that affects the affected.

➤ **EFFECTOR—EFFECTED**

The do-er can **EFFECT** a do-ee. The do-er is the **EFFECTOR**; the do-ee is the **EFFECTED**. The effector is the catalyst of an action that brings something into existence, the *effected.*

She built *the house.*

Effector *(She)* — Effected *(the house)*

She grew *grapes.*

Effector *(She)* — Effected *(grapes)*

The effector brings the effected into existence.

MENTAL = SENSING

The **MENTAL** semantic process is the verbal process of **SENSING**. Here a "**SENSE-ER**" has affection toward, cognition of, or uses the senses on a **PHE-NOMENON**. A senser is one who is able to feel (affection), to think (cognition), or to use the senses (see, hear, smell, etc.). A phenomenon is something about which a senser has feelings (affection), or thoughts (cognition), or on which a senser has used the senses.

She loves *the man.*

Senser *(She)* — Phenomenon *(the man)* = affection

204

He remembered *the story.*

Senser *(He)* — Phenomenon *(the story)* = cognition

Eli heard *Hannah's crying.*

Senser *(Eli)* — Phenomenon *(Hannah's crying)* = use of a sense

RELATIONAL = BEING

The **RELATIONAL** semantic process is the verbal process of **BEING**. We can talk of two types of relational processes.

➢ **CARRIER—ATTRIBUTE = ATTRIBUTIVE**

A **CARRIER** *carries* an **ATTRIBUTE.**

The book is *nonsense.*

Carrier *(The book)* — Attribute *(nonsense)*

The apple seems *green.*

Carrier *(The apple)* — Attribute *(green)*

The verbs tend to be an *ascriptive/descriptive* type. Here is a list of common verbs that convey an attributive semantic process.

become, turn (into), grow (into) = inception

remain, stay (as) = duration

seem, appear, qualify as, turn out, end up (as) = appearance

look, sound, smell, feel, taste (like) = sense perception

be, feel = neutral

205

➢ IDENTIFIED—IDENTIFIER = IDENTIFYING

An **IDENTIFIED** is assigned identity by an **IDENTIFIER**.

You are *the first person on earth.*

Identified *(You)* — Identifier *(the first person on earth)*

The verbs tend to be an *equative* type. Here is a list of common verbs that convey an identifying semantic process.

play, act as, function as, serve as = role

mean, indicate, suggest, imply, show, mark, reflect = sign

equal, add up to, make = equation

comprise, feature, include = kind/part

represent, constitute, form = significance

exemplify, illustrate = example

express, signify, realize, spell, stand for, mean = symbol

be, become, remain = neutral

SEMANTIC ROLES

We already have been talking about semantic **ROLES/PARTICIPANTS**. We have had to use this concept to talk about verbal processes in the last section. The concept of semantic roles or participants focuses on nouns/nominals in clauses and their relations to each other. We can divide roles/participants into those that occur as the syntactic subject of a clause and those that occur in the predicate. The chart below lists some common roles/participants in a clause.

Subject Roles	Predicate Roles
Affector	Affected
Effector	Effected
Senser	Phenomenon
Carrier	Attribute
Identified	Identifier
Processed	
	Beneficiary

In the previous section we saw examples of the roles listed in the first five rows. Here are the remaining roles:

Processed: role/participant that undergoes a process: *The apple* fell.

Beneficiary: role/participant as recipient of a benefit—positive or negative—from an action or a state/condition: He asked you for a favor *for himself.* I gave *him* the ball.

SEMANTIC CIRCUMSTANCES

Circumstances can surround verbal processes and roles/participants. English and Biblical Greek convey these circumstances primarily through adverb(ial)s and prepositional phrases. What follow are some of the common groupings of circumstances along with common structures used by English to convey the circumstance.

1) Circumstance of Extent (including interval)
   a) Distance (spatial)
      ◆ structure: noun (with modifier): He traveled *many miles.*
   b) Duration (temporal)
      ◆ structure: noun (with modifier): He slept *five days/a long time.*

207

2) Location
   a) Place (spatial)
      - structure: adverb: He lives *here/there.*
      - structure: prepositional phrase: He lives *in Galilee.*
   b) Time (temporal)
      - structure: adverb/noun (with modifier): He left *recently/a long time ago.*
      - structure: prepositional phrase: He left *at noon.*

3) Manner
   a) Means: means whereby a process takes place
      - structure: prepositional phrase: He fixed it *with rope.*
   b) Quality: characterizes the process
      - structure: adverbs: It rained *heavily.* She spoke *more calmly.*
   c) Comparison
      - structure: adverb: Aaron speaks *differently.*
      - structure: prepositional phrase: Her eyes are *like doves.*

4) Cause
   a) Reason: what causes a process
      - structure: prepositional phrase: *through, because of,* etc.: They sang *because of the rain.*
   b) Purpose: intention behind a process
      - structure: prepositional phrase: *for, for the purpose of:* They gave up land *for peace.*
   c) Behalf: who is it for?
      - structure: prepositional phrase: *for, on behalf of:* I'm writing *for/on behalf of Jeremiah.*

5) Contingency
   a) Condition
      - structure: prepositional phrase: *in the case of, in the event of:* *In the event of* fire, use water.
      - structure: particle/conjunctions: *if, unless*

   b) Concession: a circumstance conceded or granted or acknowledged
- structure: prepositional phrase: *in spite of*
- structure: particle/conjunctions: *although, though*

   c) Default
- structure: prepositional phrase: *in the absence of*

6) Accompaniment

   a) Comitative: a process represented as a single instance of a process
- Positive: *Moses and Aaron* went together. Moses went *with Aaron.* Moses set out *with his staff.*
- Negative: Moses went *without Aaron.* I got to the door *without my books.*

   b) Additive: a process represented as two or more instances
- Positive: Moses went *as well as Aaron.*
- Negative: Moses went *instead of Aaron.*

7) Role

   a) Guise: what as? He was confirmed *as high priest.*

   b) Product: what into? (what did it become?) He *became high priest.* He *grew into a man.*

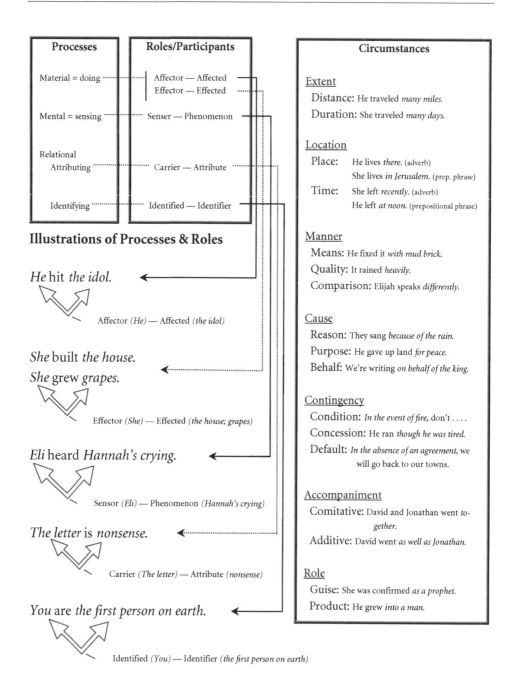

Processes	Roles/Participants	Circumstances
Material = doing	Affector — Affected	

Processes

Material = doing

Mental = sensing

Relational
  Attributing

  Identifying

Roles/Participants

Affector — Affected
Effector — Effected

Senser — Phenomenon

Carrier — Attribute

Identified — Identifier

Circumstances

<u>Extent</u>
  Distance: He traveled *many miles.*
  Duration: She traveled *many days.*

<u>Location</u>
  Place: He lives *there.* (adverb)
        She lives *in Jerusalem.* (prep. phrase)
  Time: She left *recently.* (adverb)
        He left *at noon.* (prepositional phrase)

<u>Manner</u>
  Means: He fixed it *with mud brick.*
  Quality: It rained *heavily.*
  Comparison: Elijah speaks *differently.*

<u>Cause</u>
  Reason: They sang *because of the rain.*
  Purpose: He gave up land *for peace.*
  Behalf: We're writing *on behalf of the king.*

<u>Contingency</u>
  Condition: *In the event of fire,* don't . . . .
  Concession: He ran *though he was tired.*
  Default: *In the absence of an agreement,* we
        will go back to our towns.

<u>Accompaniment</u>
  Comitative: David and Jonathan went *to-
        gether.*
  Additive: David went *as well as Jonathan.*

<u>Role</u>
  Guise: She was confirmed *as a prophet.*
  Product: He grew *into a man.*

Illustrations of Processes & Roles

He hit *the idol.*

  Affector *(He)* — Affected *(the idol)*

She built *the house.*
She grew *grapes.*

  Effector *(She)* — Effected *(the house; grapes)*

Eli heard *Hannah's crying.*

  Sensor *(Eli)* — Phenomenon *(Hannah's crying)*

The letter is *nonsense.*

  Carrier *(The letter)* — Attribute *(nonsense)*

You are *the first person on earth.*

  Identified *(You)* — Identifier *(the first person on earth)*

Figure 40: Overview of Common Processes, Roles, and Circumstances

DISCOURSE ANALYSIS

When we talk about DISCOURSE in linguistics, we are not usually referring to conversation or speech.[47] The term refers more commonly to "chunks" of text and has in mind a level of language beyond a clause isolated from another.

Discourse analysis, in short, takes seriously the notion of CONTEXT: (1) context in the sense of the interrelation of words on a page, and (2) context in the sense of space and time—a language exchange or storytelling does not occur in a vacuum. More specifically, discourse analysis notices the interplay of story and discourse, concepts I discuss below. It tracks indicators of time, location, and what a text is *about,* that is, topicality. It takes note of what is an unmarked and a marked way to write—more on this below. A somewhat more technical definition is that discourse analysis is, in part, the interface of syntax, linguistic semantics, and linguistic pragmatics.

Take a look at a photograph of a family member or friend. You are looking at that person, yet you are not. You are looking at a *representation.* Portraits present little trouble for us in this respect. We know that a portrait represents a person though it is two-dimensional and not always true to life in size and color. We recognize that a self-portrait is not real. If poked, it will not yelp. If stabbed, it will not bleed.

Writing is representation. Jesus and the disciples in the narrative writing known as the Gospels are not real people any more than a self-portrait of Vincent van Gogh is *really* or *actually* van Gogh. In saying that, however, I am not judging whether Jesus and the Twelve actually existed any more than I am calling into question whether van Gogh really lived. Jesus and his disciples in writing are not people, actual objects of genetics, but *personae,* objects of poetics and things linguistic. Discourse analysis understands that text is representation.

---

[47] Portions of this chapter first appeared in Gary A. Long, "The Written Story: Toward Understanding Text as Representation and Function," *Vetus Testamentum* 49 (1999): 165–85.

1. STORY AND DISCOURSE

When it comes to representing, it is helpful to follow a distinction made by Seymour Chatman between STORY and DISCOURSE, whether representing through written page or cinema.[48]

If you were writing a novel, the STORY would be the conceptual content in your head—the plot, the characters, settings—before you wrote it down, and it would include the conceptual content that never gets written. The DISCOURSE of that novel, however, would be the actual book I pick up to read.

If we take a person's life, your life, for example, and somebody wanted to tell others about it in written form, the STORY of your life would begin at your birth and would go from there day by day. Story would be your actual life. The DISCOURSE—the words put onto a written page in this case—however, may begin by writing about what you are doing this moment, then flash back to various periods in your lifetime and rearrange them.

2. STORY-HAPPENINGS AND DISCOURSE

The story, in the technical sense used here, is developed, in part, by HAPPENINGS, that is, fientive events (those that are *dynamic,* not static). When reading the Greek Bible (or any text), we should keep in mind that the discourse we are reading is only a representation of a story.

2.1 STORY-PRESENT, STORY-PAST, AND STORY-FUTURE

Discourse-level representation presents *perspective,* labeled STORY-PRESENT, STORY-PAST, and STORY-FUTURE. *Story-present* represents the happenings that are "at hand" in the discourse. They are the happenings that are part of a time frame that is the hub of the story. Narrative *story-past* refers to perspective that is before the happenings that are "at hand" in the discourse. Flashbacks are a prime example. Narrative *story-future* refers to perspective that is posterior to the "at hand" happenings. If, for example, I read, "Three years later Molly would discover that

---

[48] Seymour Chatman, *Story and Discourse: Narrative Structure in Fiction and Film* (Ithaca, N.Y., and London: Cornell University Press, 1978).

she had been speaking to her husband's murderer, but now she knew nothing," I have read story-future juxtaposed with story-present.

The discourse is free to rearrange the order of the actual story-happenings—the present may be juxtaposed with its past or future—and is free to spend less or more time on a story-happening than would be the time for a happening to occur in real life. Time relations of (1) order and (2) duration thus exist between story-happenings and discourse.

2.2 ORDER

Discourse may rearrange story-happenings. The discourse preserved as Mark 6:14–29 does not chronologically follow the story-happenings, the actual events. In verses 14–16, John the Baptist appears to be dead already. Verses 17–29 describe John's death.

2.3 DURATION

Duration refers, following Chatman,[49] to the relation of the time it takes to read out a discourse compared with the time the story-happenings lasted or would last.

2.3.1 Summary

Duration may, first, be summary. Here, discourse is *significantly* briefer than story-time; it compresses story-time by days, weeks, months, years, and lifetimes. Mark 1:13 reads, "He remained there for forty days." You spent no more than two seconds to read something that, if taken at face value, took forty days to accomplish.

2.3.2 Discourse-Time = Story-Time

In discourse-time = story-time, reading the discourse or text is approximate in time to what it would take for the actual situation. I mentioned above that summary representation *significantly* truncates story-time. Discourse-time = story-time, however, represents an almost precise match in time or, at most, the com-

---

[49] Chatman, *Story and Discourse*, 67–78.

pression of only a few moments. The case of dialogue between characters is a good example. The Sermon on the Mount, represented in Matthew as the sayings of Jesus on one particular day, can be read in the discourse in similar time to how Matthew wants us to understand how Jesus spoke on the hillside overlooking the Sea of Galilee (Matthew 5:3–7:27).

2.3.3 Stretch

In stretch, discourse-time is longer than story-time. In cinema this is slow motion. In recent years, a number of movies have exploited stretch effectively. The *Matrix* series, *Hero,* and *Crouching Tiger, Hidden Dragon* have thrilled us with their super slow-motion.

As an example in written discourse, albeit in the Hebrew Bible and not the Greek, we may look at Jael's killing of Sisera in the Deborah and Barak discourse preserved in Judges 4–5.

In the narrative portion, Judges 4:21, the writer represents the action in *discourse-time = story-time;* we read of Jael driving the tent peg through Sisera in the *approximate* amount of time it may have taken in real life:

> But Jael wife of Heber took a tent peg, and took a hammer in her hand, and went quietly to him and drove the peg through his mouth[50] until it went down into the ground—he was lying fast asleep from weariness—and he died.

The poetic representation of this happening, found in Judges 5:26–27, is repetitive in relation to the narrative one:

> She put her hand to the tent peg and her right hand to the mallet; she hammered a blow to Sisera, she struck his head, she hit and pierced his (open)

---

[50] The Hebrew word here translated as *mouth,* but usually translated *temple* is a rare and difficult word to understand; for *mouth* see M. Rozelaar, "An Unrecognized Part of the Human Anatomy," *Judaism* 37 (1988): 97–101, and Gary A. Long, "מקּח," in *New International Dictionary of Old Testament Theology and Exegesis* (ed. W. VanGemeren; 5 vols.; Grand Rapids, Mich.: Zondervan, 1997), 2:921–22.

mouth. He sank, he fell, he lay still at her feet; at her feet he sank, he fell; where he sank, there he fell dead.

The discourse here, in a sense, is slower than the narrative representation. It is the written equivalent of cinematic slow motion; it is s-t-r-e-t-c-h-e-d.

2.3.4 Pause

In pause, story-time stops but discourse continues. Here is where the writer describes people, scenes, and the like—things that are story-existents.[51] Matthew, immediately after telling us John the Baptist's message, puts story-time on pause and says, "John wore a garment made of camel-hair with a leather loin-cloth around his waist, and his food was locusts and wild honey" (Matthew 3:4).

3. DISCOURSE AS THE FUNCTION OF SYNTAX, SEMANTICS, AND PRAGMATICS

When working with discourse, you must realize that the functions of syntax, linguistic semantics, and pragmatics merge together in written representation. Truly grasping the conveyance of meaning comes by understanding the interrelation of these functions for a particular language.

Syntactic functions (subject, adverbial complements and adjuncts, etc.) articulate relationships and positions within a particular linguistic syntagm (that is, a string of words). *Semantic* functions specify, in part, the *meaning(s) of lexical items* (lexical semantics) and *roles* that referents may have (agent, patient, beneficiary, etc.). *Pragmatic* functions specify the informational status of part of a clause in relation to its wider contextual setting. This last function, pragmatics, affirms that natural language is carried out by humans in space and time. Language and language study, therefore, cannot be separated from humanity and human processes.

---

[51] *Story-existents* are those story components that *exist:* settings, state-of-being, characters (apart from their actions), etc.

The subsections that follow speak more about some of the major notions or ingredients that make up discourse analysis.[52] In §3.4 below, we shall see these ingredients at work in specific examples.

3.1 Topic/Topicality

A discourse is *about* something. It may, in fact, be about many things. This book, for example, is *about* basic grammatical concepts, this chapter is *about* discourse analysis, and this subsection is *about* topicality. TOPIC or TOPICALITY in pragmatics considers what an expression may be about, whether that expression is a whole discourse or an individual clause.

We are really concerned here with COHERENCE, the conceptual or emic (see under LINGUISTIC HIERARCHIES, p. 3) notion of connectivity within a story and its discourse. Related to coherence is COHESION, a label that refers to the *physically present* (= etic) discourse features involved in bringing connectivity. For discourse to be coherent, it must interface with REFERENCE FRAMES, any etic or conceptual (= emic) referent to which a discourse may refer. A reference frame may, in part, be real,[53] irreal,[54] physically present, or absent[55] in a discourse.

A discourse may have many referents or reference frames: one character, several characters, one happening, several happenings, etc. A reference frame may become a topic within a discourse. A coherent discourse must first introduce these topics—a NEW topic. Once a topic has been introduced and remains the topic, we can call it a GIVEN or ACTIVE topic. A topic that has not been mentioned for some time and is revived or reintroduced is a RESUMED topic.

---

[52] For further reading, see Simon C. Dik, *The Theory of Functional Grammar Part 1: The Structure of the Clause* (ed. Kees Hengeveld; 2d, revised ed.; Functional Grammar Series 20; Berlin: Mouton de Gruyter, 1997).

[53] That is, a reference frame may refer to phenomena that are part of the world as we know it.

[54] That is, a reference frame may refer to imaginary phenomena.

[55] For example, the utterance *Please, start walking* may have a linguistically absent reference frame (RF) of people hurriedly wanting to leave a location.

3.2 FOCUS/FOCALITY

FOCUS or FOCALITY, another feature in pragmatics, attaches importance or saliency to a reference frame. A reference frame—usually a word or phrase—that is in *focus* is one that is informationally prominent or most salient.

3.3 MARKEDNESS

In language we talk, in part, of marked features and unmarked ones: MARKEDNESS and UNMARKEDNESS—elements that fall under the scope of linguistic pragmatics. If I say, "Herod examined Jerusalem on his mount," in normal intonation, I have likely expressed an *unmarked* English syntagm (that is, a string of words). The syntax, semantics, and pragmatic features of that expression are likely normal or most typical. If, however, I say, "Herod examined Jerusalem on his *mount*," with high-falling intonation on *mount*, I have expressed a *marked* syntagm, denoting that Herod examined Jerusalem on *mount*, not by foot or by being carried. The syntax is the same. The semantic functions and meanings of the words are unchanged. The distinction between the two expressions, though, is a feature of pragmatics. I could also say, "On his *mount* Herod examined Jerusalem," with a change in syntax, the fronting of *on his mount* along with high intonation to mark the expression. We could in fact play that children's game of repeating the same expression while intonating a different word each time: "*Herod* examined Jerusalem on his mount"; "Herod *examined* . . ."; "Herod examined *Jerusalem* . . ."; etc. Each time you are expressing something meaningfully different.

Within discourse, markedness may be achieved, in part, through (1) quantity of information and (2) order or arrangement.[56]

3.3.1 Quantity of Information

Let us look first at quantity of information to denote markedness, and let us restrict ourselves here to written discourse. QUANTITY-markedness may be

---

[56] R. D. Bergen, "Text as a Guide to Authorial Intention: An Introduction to Discourse Criticism," *Journal of the Evangelical Theological Society* 30 (1987): 327–36.

achieved syntactically by the length of a clause. If a discourse that has been consistently using clauses of, let us say, X length suddenly begins using clauses longer than X, those new clauses may be marked.[57] Short, staccato-like clauses, too, may be used for markedness, particularly to mark a high point or climax of a story.

Within a large discourse, the overall length of a particular episode in relation to ones surrounding it may mark an atypical episode within the immediate textual environment. The episode preserved as Genesis 1:24–31 is more than twice the length of each of the previous five;[58] that text calls out to us, "I am marked, I am particularly important."

An important factor in deriving what is likely quantity-marked in a particular textual environment is taking note of what seems to be common in the immediate textual environment.

3.3.2 Order of Information

ORDER-markedness may be achieved, in one way, through word order in clauses—syntax. Paying attention to something as simple as whether, for example, a clause's predicate comes before or after a subject is an important initial step. In Biblical Greek, predicates tend to come after subjects, so-called S(ubject)–P(redicate) syntax. With that in mind, when in the discourse Jesus says μακάριοι οἱ πραεῖς *Blessed are the gentle* (Matthew 5:5), where the predicate μακάριοι comes first, your working assumption should be that this order is marked and conveys something meaningfully different than οἱ πραεῖς μακάριοι.

In a *written* text where we have no oral clues or other modern conventions such as capital letters, bold, or italics, the beginning of a clause is vitally important as one way of perceiving markedness within and among main clauses.

Order is not only an inner-clausal phenomenon. The order of happenings throughout an entire discourse can be very telling.

---

[57] Longer syntagms seem to be used for markedness in the Hebrew Bible at Exodus 12:29.

[58] Genesis 1:1–5 (52 words); 1:6–8 (38 words); 1:9–13 (69 words); 1:14–19 (69 words); 1:20–23 (57 words). Genesis 1:24–31 has 149 words.

3.4 MARKEDNESS FOR FOCUS AND CONNECTIVITY

Markedness may convey pragmatic FOCUS—again, the salient or prominent pragmatic information in a clause. It also plays an important role in a discourse's connectivity (coherence and cohesion). Sometimes a discourse, within its clausal structures, marks a clausal element or constituent that serves as a reference frame for guiding the recipient in tracking how clauses cohere or are grouped together:

a)   Herod examined Jerusalem on his mount.

b)   On his mount Herod examined Jerusalem.

In both (a) and (b) the notion 'mount' is a reference frame (as is 'Herod', 'Jerusalem', 'examine', plus potentially a host of absent reference frames). In (a) the reference frame represented in the phrase *on his mount* is unmarked, syntactically being placed in a normative position for English and without stressed intonation. In (b), however, the reference frame, represented in a *fronted* position within the clause, is marked. A MARKED COHESION REFERENCE FRAME (MCRF) is a label to refer to this kind of marked clausal constituent. Since a reference frame may or may not be explicitly mentioned in a discourse, the use of *cohesion* in the label refers to a reference frame being a linguistic constituent explicitly mentioned in the discourse.

These notions of focus and MCRF are here illustrated:

➢   Herod examined Jerusalem on his mount.

This example is unmarked; it is normative English. All the following examples, however, are marked in some way.

➢   Herod examined Jerusalem on his *mount* [focus]. [high-falling intonation on *mount* to mark prominent information]

➢   It was *on his mount* [focus] that Herod examined Jerusalem. [cleft clause construction and high intonation to mark prominent information]

➢   *On his mount* [focus] Herod examined Jerusalem. [fronting of the prepositional phrase and high intonation to mark prominent information]

➢ On his mount [MCRF] Herod examined Jerusalem. [normal intonation on fronted prepositional phrase; the fronted phrase—a marked construction—could here be presenting MCRF; Herod's mount could have been mentioned previously and is important somehow for discourse coherence apart from being particularly prominent]

➢ On his *mount* [focus + MCRF overlay] Herod examined Jerusalem. [fronting of the prepositional phrase and high intonation to mark prominent information (as in the previous example), and a speaker or writer might want to convey MCRF; Herod's mount could have been mentioned previously and is important somehow for discourse coherence]

3.4.1 Types of Focus[59]

Focus refers to the salient or prominent pragmatic information in a clause. It concerns the changes that a sender (speaker or writer) wants to make in the recipient's pragmatic information. Focus can be achieved, as demonstrated in part in the preceding section, through (a) prosody (e.g., intonation), (b) syntax, whether a special initial position within a clause or a special syntactic construction (e.g., a cleft construction), and (c) special focus marking words or particles.

In using focus, the sender may want to (1) fill in an assumed gap of information or (2) make a contrast. The first, **INFORMATION GAP FOCUS**, may entail the following:

(1a)   *Questioning focus,* where the sender will ask a question:

   What did you do to Jerusalem's temple? [focus marked with *wh-* interrogative construction]

(1b)   *Completive focus,* where the sender attempts to fill in an assumed information gap:

   I *refurbished* it. [focus marked with intonation]

---

[59] For further reading, see Dik, *Theory of Functional Grammar,* 309–38.

220

CONTRAST FOCUS may comprise

(2a)   *Parallel focus,* which usually highlights simultaneous or concurrent phenomena:

The Judaizers prepared their argument; *Paul* and *Peter* also prepared theirs.

(2b)   *Counter-presuppositional focus,* which embraces several more specific functions:

(2bi)   *Rejecting focus:* not A!; Paul rebuked the Corinthians. No, he didn't rebuke the *Corinthians.*

(2bii)   *Replacing focus:* (not A but) B; Paul rebuked the Corinthians. No, he rebuked the *Galatians.*

(2biii)   *Expanding focus:* also B; Paul rebuked the Corinthians. He not only rebuked the *Corinthians,* he rebuked the *Galatians.*

(2biv)   *Restricting focus:* only B; Paul rebuked the Corinthians and Galatians. No, he rebuked only the *Galatians.*

(2bv)   *Selecting focus:* (A or B) B!; Did Paul rebuke the Corinthians or Galatians? *Galatians.*

3.4.2 Types of MCRF

An MCRF, by definition, is a reference frame that is pragmatically marked. A **NewMCRF** introduces a new referent. Once a referent has been introduced and finds itself marked, it can be considered **GivenMCRF** or **ActiveMCRF**. **ResumptiveMCRF** refers to a referent that has not been mentioned for some time and is revived or reintroduced in a marked fashion.

4. STRUCTURE AND MEANING

Discourse analysis is, in part, an analysis of a discourse's STRUCTURE. We can talk of the analysis being at *micro-* and *macro-levels.* By *micro-level* I have in mind what is happening within clauses, such as the markedness or unmarkedness within them. By *macro-level* I am thinking of such things as the order of happen-

221

ings, discourse boundaries, referencing, existents (characters, places, etc.), bundles or clusters of happenings, peaks/climaxes, etc.

Discourse analysis uses a discourse's structures as *a* means (not *the* means) to arrive at MEANING. At the micro-level, having an adverbial adjunct, for example, before a main verb is *meaningful,* as is understanding possible semantic connections between clauses. At the macro-level, being concerned with the "so what?!" of a discourse is a focal point. "Okay, I've just read a discourse. So what? What is it conveying? What are its possible meanings?" Those are some of the questions of a discourse analyst.

Johannes Louw offers an interesting example of structure and meaning at a macro-level.[60] He breaks down Luke 7:36–50 into the following structure:

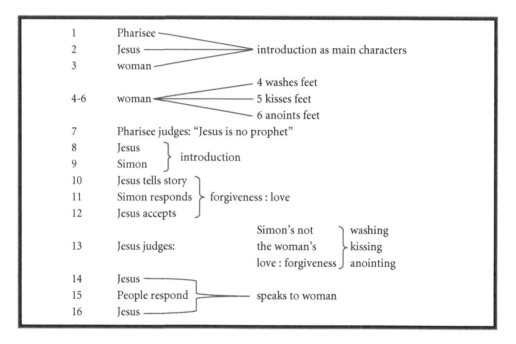

[60] Johannes Louw, "A Semiotic Approach to Discourse Analysis with Reference to Translation Theory," *Bible Translator* 36 (1985): 101–7.

When Louw stands back and asks the "so what" of this text, he believes it conveys meaningful and important irony: Jesus and his preaching is not for people (such as Pharisees) who regard themselves righteous; Jesus came to the underdog, the sinner, the outcast. Louw points out Jesus' paradoxical impact on everyday life.

5. CONCLUDING REMARK

A reader of any text, and especially of the Bible, needs to bring discourse analysis into the process. Understanding the components of a discourse goes to the core of deriving meaning(s) from a text. It ought to be a foundation of exegesis. Translation, in fact, needs to convey these meaningful elements appropriately.

Like a photograph, writing is representation. We have looked in cursory fashion at story and discourse and how the blend of syntax, semantics, and pragmatics must inform your analysis of text.

WORKS CITED

Barnwell, Katharine. *Introduction to Semantics and Translation*. 2d ed. Horsley Green, England: Summer Institute of Linguistics, 1980.

Black, David Alan. *Learn to Read New Testament Greek*. Nashville: Broadman, 1993.

_____. *Linguistics for Students of New Testament Greek: A Survey of Basic Concepts and Applications*. 2d ed. Grand Rapids, Mich.: Baker, 1995.

Blake, Barry J. *Case*. 2d ed. Cambridge Textbooks in Linguistics. Cambridge: Cambridge University Press, 2001.

Caragounis, Chrys C. *The Development of Greek and the New Testament: Morphology, Syntax, Phonology, and Textual Transmission*. Wissenschaftliche Untersuchungen zum Neuen Testament 167. Tübingen: Mohr Siebeck, 2004.

Carson, D. A. *Exegetical Fallacies*. 2d ed. Grand Rapids: Baker; Carlisle, England: Paternoster, 1996.

Chatman, Seymour. *Story and Discourse: Narrative Structure in Fiction and Film*. Ithaca, N.Y. and London: Cornell University Press, 1978.

Dik, Simon C. *The Theory of Functional Grammar Part 1: The Structure of the Clause*. Edited by Kees Hengeveld. 2d, rev. ed. Functional Grammar Series 20. Berlin: Mouton de Gruyter, 1997.

Halliday, M. A. K. *An Introduction to Functional Grammar*. 2d ed. London: Arnold, 1994.

Kemmer, Suzanne. *The Middle Voice*. Typological Studies in Language 23. Amsterdam and Philadelphia: John Benjamins, 1993.

Long, Gary A. *Grammatical Concepts 101 for Biblical Hebrew: Learning Biblical Hebrew Grammatical Concepts through English Grammar*. Peabody, Mass.: Hendrickson, 2002.

_____. "מָחַק." Pages 921–22 in vol. 2 of *New International Dictionary of Old Testament Theology and Exegesis*. Edited by W. VanGemeren. 5 vols. Grand Rapids, Mich.: Zondervan, 1997.

_____. "The Written Story: Toward Understanding Text as Representation and Function." *Vetus Testamentum* 49 (1999): 165–85.

Louw, Johannes. "A Semiotic Approach to Discourse Analysis with Reference to Translation Theory." *Bible Translator* 36 (1985): 101–107.

Lyons, John. *Introduction to Theoretical Linguistics*. Cambridge: Cambridge University Press, 1968.

Mounce, William D. *Basics of Biblical Greek: Grammar*. Grand Rapids, Mich.: Zondervan, 1993.

Porter, Stanley E. *Idioms of the Greek New Testament*. 2d ed. Biblical Languages: Greek 2. Sheffield, England: Sheffield Academic Press, 1994.

_____. *Verbal Aspect in the Greek of the New Testament, with Reference to Tense and Mood*. Studies in Biblical Greek 1. New York: Peter Lang, 1989.

Robertson, A. T. *A Grammar of the Greek New Testament in the Light of Historical Research*. 5th ed. New York: Richard R. Smith; London: Hodder & Stoughton, 1931.

Rozelaar, M. "An Unrecognized Part of the Human Anatomy," *Judaism* 37 (1988): 97–101.

Smyth, Herbert Weir. *Greek Grammar*. Revised by Gordon M. Messing. Cambridge: Harvard University Press, 1956.

Stevens, Gerald L. *New Testament Greek*. 2d ed. Lanham, Md.: University Press of America, 1997.

Summers, Ray. *Essentials of New Testament Greek*. Revised by Thomas Sawyer. Rev. ed. Nashville: Broadman & Holman, 1995.

Turner, Nigel. *Syntax*. Vol. 3 of James Hope Moulton, *A Grammar of New Testament Greek*. Edinburgh: T&T Clark, 1963.

Wallace, Daniel B. *The Basics of New Testament Syntax: An Intermediate Greek Grammar*. Grand Rapids, Mich.: Zondervan, 2000.

_____. *Greek Grammar beyond the Basics: An Exegetical Syntax of the New Testament.* Grand Rapids, Mich.: Zondervan, 1996.

INDEX OF TOPICS

Greek, 108, 138, 166
  anarthrous, 41, 111, 156
  arthrous/articular, 41, 109, 148
articular. *See* arthrous/articular
aspect, 57, 60, 61, 68, 62, 64, 65, 68, 70, 71, 183
  definition of, 62
  imperfective, 62, 65, 71, 72, 73, 74, 75, 79, 90
    definition of, 64
  perfective, 62, 63, 64, 65, 66, 67, 71, 73, 74, 75, 77, 79, 90
    definition of, 62
  resultative/stative, 62, 66, 73, 76
    definition of, 66
attribute, 158, 159, 160, 169, 170, 205
attribute as semantic role. *See* role, as semantic concept, attribute
attributive adjective. *See* adjective, attributive descriptive
attributive relative clause. *See* relative clause, Greek, dependent/attributive
auxiliary verb. *See* verb, auxiliary

B

basilect, xxi, 85
beneficiary as semantic role. *See* role, as semantic concept, beneficiary
bilabial, 8
British English, 32, 33

C

carrier as semantic role. *See* role, as semantic concept, carrier
case, xix, 56, 37, 108, 143, 144, 150, 153, 156, 164, 166, 169, 170, 171, 175, 183, 188, 199
  English
    nonpossessive case (for nouns), 34
    normal/common case (for nouns), 34
    object case (for pronouns), 34, 35, 50, 123, 130, 133

    possessive case (for nouns and pronouns), 34, 35, 36, 130, 132
    predicate nominative, 35, 187
    subject case (for pronouns), 34, 35, 122, 130, 133
  Greek
    ablative, 36, 37
    accusative, 34, 36, 37, 38, 44, 50, 54, 133, 134, 150, 155
      apposition accusative, 45, 49
      as adverbial adjunct, 44, 45, 47, 48, 49, 51, 195, 197, 202. *See* also adverbial adjunct, accusative as
      as adverbial complement, 44, 45, 46, 47, 49, 53, 56, 195, 202. *See* also adverbial complement, accusative as
      independent accusative, 45, 50
      pendent/hanging accusative, 45, 50
      subject accusative, 45, 48
    dative, 34, 36, 37, 38, 48, 50, 54, 136, 150, 155
      as adverbial adjunct, 54, 197, 202. *See* also adverbial adjunct, dative as
      associative dative
        dative of indirect object, 55
        instrumental dative, 55
        locative dative, 55
      as adverbial complement, 54, 56, 202. *See* also adverbial complement, dative as
    genitive, 34, 36, 37, 38, 50, 54, 135, 136, 140, 142, 150, 155, 169, 170
      adjective genitive, 51, 52
      adverbial genitive, 51, 52
      subject genitive, 51, 52
      verb-governed genitive, 51, 53, 54, 202
        adverbial adjunct, 53. *See* also adverbial adjunct, genitive as

English
    as adverbial adjunct, 188
    as adverbial complement, 188
    as predicate nominative, 187
    as subject, 187
Greek
    as adverbial adjunct, 189
    as adverbial complement, 189
    as subject, 189
inflection, xxi, 29, 109 *See* also declension
information gap focus. *See* focus/focality,
    information gap
initiator as semantic role. *See* role, as
    semantic concept, initiator
instrument as semantic circumstance. *See*
    circumstance as semantic concept,
    instrument
intensity as semantic circumstance. *See*
    circumstance as semantic concept,
    intensity
interdental, 8
internal accusative. *See* adverbial
    complement, accusative as
interrogative adjective. *See* adjective,
    interrogative
interrogative pronoun. *See* pronoun,
    interrogative
intonation, 217, 219, 220
    for markedness, 217, 219, 220
intransitive. *See* verb,
    intransitive/intransitivity
iota subscript, 16, 33
irreal mood. *See* mood/modality
iterativity. *See* verb, iterativity

J

juxtaposition, 40, 42, 166, 200, 201, 213

L

labial, 8
labioalveolar, 8
labiodental, 8

labiovelar, 8, 13, 16
lateral, 11
lex/lexeme, 3, 4, 5, 21
linking verb. *See* verb, linking
liquid, 11
location as semantic circumstance. *See*
    circumstance as semantic concept,
    location

M

main clause. *See* clause, independent/main
    as different from independent clause, 193
manner as semantic circumstance. *See*
    circumstance as semantic concept,
    manner
manner of articulation, 8, 9
marked. *See* markedness
marked cohesion reference frame (MCRF),
    219, 220, 221
    Given/ActiveMCRF, 221
    NewMCRF, 221
    ResumptiveMCRF, 221
markedness, 93, 211, 217, 218, 219, 220, 221
    intonation as. *See* intonation, for
        markedness
    order, 217, 218
    quantity, 217, 218
MCRF. *See* marked cohesion reference frame
    (MCRF)
middle voice. *See* voice
"modal". *See* mood/modality
modal auxiliary, 82, 87
monophthong. *See* vowel, simple/pure
monophthongize, 16
mood/modality, 57, 71, 78, 81
    English
        irreal, 81
            nonvolitional, 81, 84
                "modal", 82
                subjunctive, 85, 86, 87
            volitional, 78, 81, 83
                2d person = imperative, 78, 79,
                    83, 84

233